Xenophon, Robert West Taylor

Xenophon's Agesilaus

With Syntax Rules and References, Notes and Indices

Xenophon, Robert West Taylor

Xenophon's Agesilaus
With Syntax Rules and References, Notes and Indices

ISBN/EAN: 9783337157630

Printed in Europe, USA, Canada, Australia, Japan

Cover: Foto ©Thomas Meinert / pixelio.de

More available books at **www.hansebooks.com**

XENOPHON'S

AGESILAUS

WITH SYNTAX RULES AND REFERENCES

NOTES AND INDICES

BY

R. W. TAYLOR, M.A.

HEAD-MASTER OF KELLY COLLEGE, TAVISTOCK
AND FORMERLY FELLOW OF ST. JOHN'S COLLEGE, CAMBRIDGE

RIVINGTONS

WATERLOO PLACE, LONDON

𝕺𝖝𝖋𝖔𝖗𝖉 𝖆𝖓𝖉 𝕮𝖆𝖒𝖇𝖗𝖎𝖉𝖌𝖊

MDCCCLXXX

CONTENTS.

ΞΕΝΟΦΩΝΤΟΣ ΑΓΗΣΙΛΑΟΣ.

CHAPTER I.

AGESILAUS IN ASIA.

Noble descent of Agesilaus, the noblest of the noblest city in Greece.

1. Οἶδα μὲν ὅτι⁴³ᵇ τῆς Ἀγησιλάου ἀρετῆς τε καὶ δόξης οὐ ῥᾴδιον ἄξιον ἔπαινον γράψαι,²⁹ᵃ ὅμως δ᾽ ἐγχειρητέον. οὐ γὰρ ἂν καλῶς ἔχοι⁵³ᵇ εἰ, ὅτι τελέως ἀνὴρ ἀγαθὸς ἐγένετο,⁵¹ διὰ τοῦτο οὐδὲ μειόνων ἂν τυγχάνοι⁵⁴ᵇ ἐπαίνων.²³ 2. περὶ μὲν οὖν εὐγενείας αὐτοῦ τί ἄν τις μεῖζον καὶ κάλλιον εἰπεῖν ἔχοι ἢ ὅτι ἔτι καὶ νῦν τοῖς προγόνοις ὀνομαζομένοις¹⁹ᵃ,⁶⁰ ἀπομνημονεύεται, ὁπόστος ἀφ᾽ Ἡρακλέους ἐγένετο,⁴⁵ καὶ τούτοις οὐκ ἰδιώταις ἀλλ᾽ ἐκ βασιλέων βασιλεῦσιν ; 3. ἀλλὰ μὴν οὐδὲ ταύτῃ γ᾽ ἄν τις ἔχοι⁵⁴ᵇ καταμέμψασθαι²⁹ᵃ αὐτοὺς ὡς βασιλεύουσι μέν,⁴³ᵇ πόλεως²⁵ δὲ τῆς ἐπιτυχούσης· ἀλλ᾽ ὥσπερ τὸ γένος αὐτῶν τῆς πατρίδος ἐντιμότατον, οὕτω καὶ ἡ πόλις ἐν τῇ Ἑλλάδι ἐνδοξοτάτη· ὥστε οὐ δευτέρων²⁵ πρωτεύουσιν, ἀλλ᾽ ἡγεμόνων ἡγεμονεύουσι.

The worth of the kingly race is shown by the permanence of the monarchy in Sparta.

4. τῇδέ γε μὴν καὶ κοινῇ ἄξιον ἐπαινέσαι τήν τε πατρίδα καὶ τὸ γένος αὐτοῦ· ἥ τε γὰρ πόλις οὐδεπώποτε φθονήσασα τοῦ²³ προτετιμῆσθαι αὐτοὺς ἐπεχείρησε καταλῦσαι²⁹ᵃ τὴν ἀρχὴν αὐτῶν, οἵ τε βασιλεῖς οὐδεπώποτε μειζόνων²³ ὠρέχθησαν ἢ ἐφ᾽ οἷσπερ ἐξ ἀρχῆς τὴν βασι-

λείαν παρέλαβον. τοιγαροῦν ἄλλη μὲν οὐδεμία ἀρχὴ
φανερά ἐστι διαγεγενημένη[59] ἀδιάσπαστος οὔτε δημο-
κρατία οὔτε ὀλιγαρχία οὔτε τυραννὶς οὔτε βασιλεία· αὕτη
δὲ μόνη διαμένει συνεχὴς βασιλεία.

The personal merit which gained him the kingdom.

5. Ὥς γε μὴν καὶ πρὶν ἄρξαι[52a] ἄξιος τῆς βασιλείας
ἐδόκει εἶναι Ἀγησίλαος τάδε τὰ[5a] σημεῖα. ἐπεὶ γὰρ
Ἄγις βασιλεὺς ὢν ἐτελεύτησεν, ἐρισάντων[27] περὶ τῆς
ἀρχῆς Λεωτυχίδα[3] μὲν ὡς Ἄγιδος ὄντος υἱοῦ, Ἀγησιλάου
δὲ ὡς Ἀρχιδάμου, κρίνασα ἡ πόλις ἀνεπικλητότερον
εἶναι[43a] Ἀγησίλαον καὶ τῷ γένει[19a] καὶ τῇ ἀρετῇ τοῦτον
ἐστήσατο βασιλέα.[5a] καίτοι τὸ ἐν τῇ κρατίστῃ πόλει
ὑπὸ τῶν ἀρίστων κριθέντα τοῦ καλλίστου γέρως[25a]
ἀξιωθῆναι[30] ποίων ἔτι τεκμηρίων[26a] προσδεῖται τῆς γε
πρὶν ἄρξαι αὐτὸν ἀρετῆς ;[8]

*Soon after his accession he volunteers to cross over into Asia, and
to assume the offensive against the Persian forces, so as to
secure Greece from invasion.*

6. Ὅσα γε μὴν ἐν τῇ βασιλείᾳ διεπράξατο[43] νῦν ἤδη
διηγήσομαι· ἀπὸ γὰρ τῶν ἔργων καὶ τοὺς τρόπους αὐτοῦ
κάλλιστα νομίζω καταδήλους ἔσεσθαι. Ἀγησίλαος τοίνυν
ἔτι μὲν νέος ὢν[58b] ἔτυχε τῆς βασιλείας·[23] ἄρτι δὲ ὄντος
αὐτοῦ ἐν τῇ ἀρχῇ, ἐξηγγέλθη βασιλεὺς ὁ Περσῶν ἀθροί-
ζων[43c] καὶ ναυτικὸν καὶ πεζὸν πολὺ στράτευμα ὡς ἐπὶ
τοὺς Ἕλληνας· 7. βουλευομένων δὲ περὶ τούτων Λακεδαιμονίων καὶ τῶν συμμάχων, Ἀγησίλαος ὑπέστη, ἐὰν
δῶσιν[53b,47] αὐτῷ τριάκοντα μὲν Σπαρτιατῶν, δισχιλίους δὲ
νεοδαμώδεις, εἰς ἑξακισχιλίους δὲ τὸ σύνταγμα τῶν συμμάχων, διαβήσεσθαι[43a] εἰς τὴν Ἀσίαν καὶ πειράσεσθαι
εἰρήνην ποιῆσαι,[29c] ἢ ἂν πολεμεῖν βούληται ὁ βάρβαρος,

6

ἀσχολίαν αὐτῷ παρέξειν στρατεύειν[29d] ἐπὶ τοὺς Ἕλληνας·
8. εὐθὺς μὲν οὖν πολλοὶ πάνυ ἠγάσθησαν αὐτὸ τοῦτο τὸ
ἐπιθυμῆσαι, ἐπειδὴ ὁ Πέρσης πρόσθεν ἐπὶ τὴν Ἑλλάδα
διέβη, ἀντιδιαβῆναι ἐπ᾽ αὐτόν, τό τε αἱρεῖσθαι ἐπιόντα[29b]
μᾶλλον ἢ ὑπομένοντα μάχεσθαι αὐτῷ, καὶ τὸ τἀκείνου
δαπανῶντα βούλεσθαι μᾶλλον ἢ τὰ τῶν Ἑλλήνων πολεμεῖν, κάλλιστον δὲ πάντων ἐκρίνετο μὴ περὶ τῆς Ἑλλάδος
ἀλλὰ περὶ τῆς Ἀσίας τὸν ἀγῶνα καθιστάναι.[29a]

Tissaphernes' treachery and Agesilaus' good faith.

9. Ἐπεὶ γε μὴν λαβὼν[58b] τὸ στράτευμα ἐξέπλευσε,
πῶς ἄν τις σαφέστερον ἐπιδείξειεν[53c] ὡς ἐστρατήγησεν ἢ εἰ
αὐτὰ διηγήσαιτο ἃ ἔπραξεν ; 10. ἐν τοίνυν τῇ Ἀσίᾳ ἥδε
πρώτη πρᾶξις[5] ἐγένετο· Τισσαφέρνης μὲν ὤμοσεν Ἀγησιλάῳ,[16] εἰ σπείσαιτο ἕως ἔλθοιεν[52] οὓς πέμψειε[48] πρὸς
βασιλέα ἀγγέλους, διαπράξεσθαι αὐτῷ ἀφεθῆναι[29b] αὐτο-
νόμους[5] τὰς ἐν τῇ Ἀσίᾳ πόλεις Ἑλληνίδας, Ἀγησίλαος
δὲ ἀντώμοσε σπονδὰς ἄξειν[43a] ἀδόλως, ὁρισάμενος τῆς
πράξεως τρεῖς μῆνας. 11. ὁ μὲν δὴ Τισσαφέρνης ἃ ὤμοσεν
εὐθὺς ἐψεύσατο. ἀντὶ γὰρ τοῦ εἰρήνην πράττειν[30] στράτευμα πολὺ παρὰ βασιλέως πρὸς ᾧ[4a] πρόσθεν εἶχε μετεπέμπετο. Ἀγησίλαος δὲ καίπερ αἰσθόμενος[58d] ταῦτα
ὅμως ἐνέμεινε ταῖς σπονδαῖς.[15] 12. ἐμοὶ οὖν τοῦτο πρῶτον
καλὸν δοκεῖ διαπράξασθαι[29c] ὅτι Τισσαφέρνην μὲν ἐμφανίσας ἐπίορκον ἄπιστον πᾶσιν ἐποίησεν, ἑαυτὸν δ᾽ ἀντ-
επιδείξας πρῶτον μὲν ὅρκους ἐμπεδοῦντα,[43c] ἔπειτα συνθή-
κας μὴ ψευδόμενον, πάντας ἐποίησε καὶ Ἕλληνας καὶ
βαρβάρους θαρροῦντας συντίθεσθαι ἑαυτῷ, εἴ τι βούλοιτο.

Tissaphernes declares war.

13. Ἐπεὶ δὲ μέγα φρονήσας[58a,f] ὁ Τισσαφέρνης ἐπὶ τῷ
καταβάντι στρατεύματι προεῖπεν Ἀγησιλάῳ[16] πόλεμον,

εἰ μὴ ἀπίοι[53e] ἐκ τῆς ᾿Ασίας, οἱ μὲν ἄλλοι σύμμαχοι καὶ
Λακεδαιμονίων οἱ παρόντες μάλα ἀχθεσθέντες[59] φανεροὶ
ἐγένοντο, νομίζοντες[58a] μείονα τὴν παροῦσαν δύναμιν[5]
᾿Αγησιλάῳ τῆς βασιλέως παρασκευῆς εἶναι· ᾿Αγησίλαος
δὲ μάλα φαιδρῷ τῷ προσώπῳ[5a] ἀπαγγεῖλαι τῷ Τισ-
σαφέρνει τοὺς πρέσβεις ἐκέλευσεν ὡς πολλὴν χάριν αὐτῷ
ἔχοι[43b] ὅτι ἐπιορκήσας[58f] αὐτὸς μὲν πολεμίους τοὺς θεοὺς
ἐκτήσατο,[47] τοῖς δ᾿ ῞Ελλησι[16] συμμάχους ἐποίησεν.

Tissaphernes is put on a false scent and outwitted.

14. ἐκ δὲ τούτου εὐθὺς τοῖς μὲν στρατιώταις[16] παρήγγειλε συσκευάζεσθαι[44] ὡς εἰς στρατείαν· ταῖς δὲ πόλεσιν
εἰς ἃς ἀνάγκη ἦν ἀφικνεῖσθαι στρατευομένῳ[58b] ἐπὶ Καρίαν
προεῖπεν ἀγορὰν παρασκευάζειν. ἐπέστειλε δὲ καὶ ῎Ιωσι
καὶ Αἰολεῦσι καὶ ῾Ελλησποντίοις πέμπειν πρὸς αὐτὸν εἰς
῎Εφεσον τοὺς συστρατευσομένους.[50a] 15. ὁ μὲν οὖν Τισσαφέρνης, καὶ ὅτι ἱππικὸν οὐκ εἶχεν[51] ὁ ᾿Αγησίλαος, ἡ δὲ
Καρία ἄφιππος ἦν, καὶ ὅτι ἡγεῖτο αὐτὸν ὀργίζεσθαι[43a]
αὐτῷ[16] διὰ τὴν ἀπάτην, τῷ ὄντι νομίσας ἐπὶ τὸν αὐτοῦ
οἶκον εἰς Καρίαν ὁρμήσειν αὐτόν, τὸ μὲν πεζὸν ἅπαν[5]
διεβίβασεν ἐκεῖσε, τὸ δὲ ἱππικὸν εἰς τὸ Μαιάνδρου πεδίον
περιήγαγε, νομίζων ἱκανὸς[9] εἶναι καταπατῆσαι τῇ ἵππῳ
τοὺς ῞Ελληνας πρὶν εἰς τὰ δύσιππα ἀφικέσθαι. 16. ὁ δὲ
᾿Αγησίλαος ἀντὶ τοῦ ἐπὶ Καρίαν ἰέναι[30] εὐθὺς ἀντιστρέψας
ἐπὶ Φρυγίας[23] ἐπορεύετο· καὶ τάς τε ἐν τῇ πορείᾳ ἀπαντώσας δυνάμεις[8] ἀναλαμβάνων ἦγε καὶ τὰς πόλεις κατ-
εστρέφετο καὶ ἐμβαλὼν ἀπροσδοκήτως παμπληθῆ
χρήματα ἔλαβε. 17. στρατηγικὸν οὖν καὶ τοῦτο ἐδόκει
διαπράξασθαι ὅτι ἐπεὶ πόλεμος προερρήθη[52] καὶ τὸ ἐξαπατᾶν ὅσιόν τε καὶ δίκαιον ἐξ ἐκείνου ἐγένετο, παῖδα
ἀπέδειξε τὸν Τισσαφέρνην τῇ ἀπάτῃ,[19a] φρονίμως δὲ καὶ
τοὺς φίλους ἐνταῦθα ἔδοξε πλουτίσαι.

Agesilaus looks to his friends' interest in the sale of the spoil.

18. Ἐπεὶ γὰρ διὰ τὸ πολλὰ χρήματα εἰλῆφθαι[30] ἀντίπροικα τὰ πάντα ἐπωλεῖτο,[1a] τοῖς μὲν φίλοις προεῖπεν ὠνεῖσθαι,[44] εἰπὼν ὅτι καταβήσοιτο[43b] ἐπὶ θάλατταν ἐν τάχει τὸ στράτευμα κατάγων·[58f] τοὺς δὲ λαφυροπώλας ἐκέλευσε γραφομένους ὁπόσου[25a] τι πρίαιντο προΐεσθαι τὰ χρήματα. ὥστε οὐδὲν προτελέσαντες[58f] οἱ φίλοι αὐτοῦ οὐδὲ τὸ δημόσιον βλάψαντες πάντες παμπληθῆ χρήματα ἔλαβον.[49a] 19. ἔτι δὲ ὁπότε αὐτόμολοι ὡς εἰκὸς πρὸς βασιλέα ἰόντες χρήματα ἐθέλοιεν[52, 40b] ὑφηγεῖσθαι, καὶ ταῦτα ἐπεμέλετο ὡς διὰ τῶν φίλων ἁλίσκοιτο,[50e] ὅπως ἅμα μὲν χρηματίζοιντο, ἅμα δὲ ἐνδοξότεροι γίγνοιντο. διὰ μὲν δὴ ταῦτα εὐθὺς πολλοὺς ἐραστὰς τῆς αὑτοῦ φιλίας ἐποιήσατο.

His clemency towards his enemies, and dislike of harsh measures.

20. Γιγνώσκων δ' ὅτι ἡ μὲν πορθουμένη[32, 58c] καὶ ἐρημουμένη χώρα οὐκ ἂν δύναιτο[53c] πολὺν χρόνον[14a] στράτευμα φέρειν, ἡ δ' οἰκουμένη μὲν σπειρομένη δὲ ἀέναον ἂν τὴν τροφὴν[5] παρέχοι, ἐπεμέλετο οὐ μόνον τοῦ βίᾳ χειροῦσθαι[23] τοὺς ἐναντίους, ἀλλὰ καὶ τοῦ πραότητι[19a] προσάγεσθαι. 21. καὶ πολλάκις μὲν προηγόρευε τοῖς στρατιώταις[18] τοὺς ἁλισκομένους μὴ[62a] ὡς ἀδίκους τιμωρεῖσθαι, ἀλλ' ὡς ἀνθρώπους ὄντας φυλάττειν, πολλάκις δὲ ὁπότε μεταστρατοπεδεύοιτο, εἰ αἴσθοιτο[40b] καταλελειμμένα παιδάρια παρὰ ἐμπόρων, ἃ πολλοὶ ἐπώλουν διὰ τὸ νομίζειν μὴ δύνασθαι ἂν φέρειν αὐτὰ καὶ τρέφειν, ἐπεμέλετο καὶ τούτων ὅπως συγκομίζοιντό[50e] ποι. 22. τοῖς δ' αὖ διὰ γῆρας καταλειπομένοις αἰχμαλώτοις[8] προσέταττεν ἐπιμελεῖσθαι αὐτῶν, ὡς μήτε ὑπὸ κυνῶν μήθ' ὑπὸ λύκων διαφθείροιντο. ὥστε οὐ μόνον οἱ[8a] πυνθανόμενοι ταῦτα, ·

B　　　　9

ἀλλὰ καὶ αὐτοὶ οἱ ἁλισκόμενοι εὐμενεῖς αὐτῷ ἐγίγνοντο.[49a]
ὁπόσας δὲ πόλεις προσάγοιτο,[48] ἀφαιρῶν αὐτῶν ὅσα[13]
δοῦλοι δεσπόταις[16] ὑπηρετοῦσι προσέταττεν ὅσα ἐλεύθεροι
ἄρχουσι πείθονται· καὶ τῶν κατὰ κράτος ἀναλώτων
τειχέων[21b] τῇ φιλανθρωπίᾳ ὑπὸ χεῖρα[66] ἐποιεῖτο.

How Agesilaus provided himself with cavalry.

23. Ἐπεὶ μέντοι ἀνὰ τὰ πεδία οὐδὲ ἐν τῇ Φρυγίᾳ
ἐδύνατο στρατεύεσθαι διὰ τὴν Φαρναβάζου ἱππείαν, ἔδοξεν
αὐτῷ ἱππικὸν κατασκευαστέον[31] εἶναι, ὡς μὴ δραπετεύοντα
πολεμεῖν δέοι[50] αὐτόν. τοὺς μὲν οὖν πλουσιωτάτους ἐκ
πασῶν τῶν ἐκεῖ πόλεων[2] ἱπποτροφεῖν[29d] κατέλεξε. 24.
προεῖπε δέ, ὅστις παρέχοιτο[48] ἵππον καὶ ὅπλα καὶ ἄνδρα
δόκιμον, ὡς ἐξέσοιτο[43b] αὐτῷ μὴ[62] στρατεύεσθαι· καὶ
ἐποίησεν οὕτως ἕκαστον προθύμως ταῦτα πράττειν[29a]
ὥσπερ ἄν τις τὸν ὑπὲρ αὐτοῦ ἀποθανούμενον προθύμως
μαστεύοι,[54b] ἔταξε δὲ καὶ πόλεις ἐξ ὧν δέοι[43] τοὺς ἱππέας
παρασκευάζειν, νομίζων ἐκ τῶν ἱπποτρόφων πόλεων εὐθὺς
καὶ φρονηματίας μάλιστα ἂν ἐπὶ τῇ ἱππικῇ γενέσθαι.[55]
καὶ τοῦτ᾽ οὖν ἀγαστῶς ἔδοξε πρᾶξαι ὅτι κατεσκεύαστο τὸ
ἱππικὸν αὐτῷ καὶ εὐθὺς ἐρρωμένον ἦν καὶ ἐνεργόν.

*Gathering and training of the army at Ephesus. How Agesilaus
stirred the enthusiasm of his soldiers.*

25. ἐπειδὴ δὲ ἔαρ ὑπέφαινε,[52] συνήγαγε πᾶν τὸ στράτευμα εἰς Ἔφεσον· ἀσκῆσαι δὲ αὐτὸ βουλόμενος ἆθλα
προὔθηκε καὶ ταῖς ἱππικαῖς τάξεσιν, ἥτις κράτιστα
ἱππεύοι,[40b] καὶ ταῖς ὁπλιτικαῖς, ἥτις ἄριστα σωμάτων
ἔχοι· καὶ πελτασταῖς δὲ καὶ τοξόταις ἆθλα προὔθηκεν,
οἵτινες κράτιστοι τὰ προσήκοντα ἔργα[13] φαίνοιντο. ἐκ
τούτου δὲ παρῆν ὁρᾶν[29a] τὰ μὲν γυμνάσια[5] μεστὰ τῶν
ἀνδρῶν γυμναζομένων, τὸν δὲ ἱππόδρομον ἱππέων ἱππαζο-

μένων, τοὺς δὲ ἀκοντιστὰς καὶ τοὺς τοξότας ἐπὶ στόχον ἱέντας. 26. ἀξίαν δὲ καὶ ὅλην τὴν πόλιν ἐν ᾗ ἦν θέας²⁵ᵃ ἐποίησεν. ἥ τε γὰρ ἀγορὰ μεστὴ ἦν παντοδαπῶν καὶ ὅπλων²⁶ᵃ καὶ ἵππων ὠνίων, οἵ τε χαλκοτύποι καὶ οἱ τέκτονες καὶ οἱ σιδηρεῖς καὶ σκυτεῖς καὶ γραφεῖς πάντες πολεμικὰ ὅπλα κατεσκεύαζον· ὥστε τὴν πόλιν ὄντως ἂν ἡγήσω⁴⁹ᵃˋ⁵⁴ᵇ πολέμου ἐργαστήριον εἶναι. 27. ἐπερρώσθη δ' ἄν τις κἀκεῖνο ἰδών,⁵⁸ᶜ Ἀγησίλαον μὲν πρῶτον, ἔπειτα δὲ καὶ τοὺς ἄλλους στρατιώτας ἐστεφανωμένους τε ὅπου ἀπὸ τῶν γυμνασίων ἴοιεν,⁴⁰ᵇ καὶ ἀνατιθέντας τοὺς στεφάνους τῇ Ἀρτέμιδι. ὅπου γὰρ ἄνδρες θεοὺς μὲν σέβοιεν, πολεμικὰ δὲ ἀσκοῖεν, πειθαρχίαν δὲ μελετῷεν, πῶς οὐκ εἰκὸς ἐνταῦθα πάντα μεστὰ ἐλπίδων²⁶ᵃ ἀγαθῶν εἶναι ;

He makes them feel contempt for their foes by a strange device.

28. Ἡγούμενος δὲ καὶ τὸ καταφρονεῖν τῶν πολεμίων²⁵ ῥώμην τινὰ ἐμβαλεῖν πρὸς τὸ μάχεσθαι, προεῖπε τοῖς κήρυξι τοὺς ὑπὸ τῶν λῃστῶν ἁλισκομένους βαρβάρους⁸ γυμνοὺς⁵ πωλεῖν. ὁρῶντες οὖν οἱ στρατιῶται λευκοὺς μὲν διὰ τὸ μηδέποτε ἐκδύεσθαι,³⁰ πίονας δὲ καὶ ἀπόνους διὰ τὸ ἀεὶ ἐπ' ὀχημάτων εἶναι, ἐνόμισαν μηδὲν διοίσειν τὸν πόλεμον ἢ εἰ γυναιξὶ δέοι⁵⁵ˋ³⁷ᵃ μάχεσθαι. προεῖπε δὲ καὶ τοῦτο τοῖς στρατιώταις ὡς εὐθὺς ἡγήσοιτο τὴν συντομωτάτην¹⁰ ἐπὶ τὰ κράτιστα τῆς χώρας,²⁵ ὅπως αὐτόθεν αὐτῷ τὰ σώματα καὶ τὴν γνώμην παρασκευάζοιντο ὡς ἀγωνιούμενοι.⁵⁰ᵃ

The advance upon Sardis.

29. Ὁ μέντοι Τισσαφέρνης ταῦτα μὲν ἐνόμισε λέγειν αὐτὸν⁴³ᵃ πάλιν βουλόμενον ἐξαπατῆσαι, εἰς Καρίαν δὲ νῦν τῷ ὄντι ἐμβαλεῖν. τό τε οὖν πεζὸν⁸ᵃ καθάπερ τὸ πρόσθεν εἰς Καρίαν διεβίβασε, καὶ τὸ ἱππικὸν εἰς τὸ Μαιάνδρου πεδίον κατέστησεν. ὁ δὲ Ἀγησίλαος οὐκ ἐψεύσατο, ἀλλ'

ὥσπερ προεῖπεν εὐθὺς ἐπὶ τὸν Σαρδιανὸν τόπον ἐχώρησε, καὶ τρεῖς μὲν ἡμέρας[14a] δι' ἐρημίας πολεμίων[25a] πορευόμενος πολλὰ[5] τὰ ἐπιτήδεια τῇ στρατιᾷ παρεῖχε· τῇ δὲ τετάρτῃ ἡμέρᾳ[19c] ἧκον οἱ τῶν πολεμίων ἱππεῖς. 30. καὶ τῷ μὲν ἄρχοντι τῶν σκευοφόρων εἶπεν ὁ ἡγεμὼν διαβάντι[18] τὸν Πακτωλὸν ποταμὸν στρατοπεδεύεσθαι· αὐτοὶ δὲ κατιδόντες τοὺς τῶν Ἑλλήνων ἀκολούθους ἐσπαρμένους καθ' ἁρπαγὴν πολλοὺς αὐτῶν ἀπέκτειναν.

Finding the enemy unprepared, he gives them battle, and takes their camp. He then marches on Sardis.

Αἰσθόμενος δὲ ὁ Ἀγησίλαος βοηθεῖν[44] ἐκέλευσε τοὺς ἱππέας. οἱ δ' αὖ Πέρσαι ὡς εἶδον τὴν βοήθειαν, ἠθροίσθησαν καὶ ἀντιπαρετάξαντο παμπληθέσι τῶν ἱππέων τάξεσιν.[19a] 31. ἔνθα δὴ ὁ Ἀγησίλαος γιγνώσκων ὅτι τοῖς μὲν πολεμίοις οὔπω παρείη[43b] τὸ πεζόν, αὐτῷ[17] δὲ οὐδὲν ἀπείη τῶν παρεσκευασμένων,[21] καιρὸν ἡγήσατο μάχην συνάψαι,[29d] εἰ δύναιτο. σφαγιασάμενος οὖν τὴν μὲν φάλαγγα εὐθὺς ἦγεν ἐπὶ τοὺς ἀντιτεταγμένους ἱππέας, ἐκ δὲ τῶν ὁπλιτῶν ἐκέλευσε τὰ δέκα ἀφ' ἥβης θεῖν ὁμόσε αὐτοῖς,[16] τοῖς δὲ πελτασταῖς εἶπε δρόμῳ ὑφηγεῖσθαι· παρήγγειλε δὲ καὶ τοῖς ἱππεῦσιν ἐμβάλλειν, ὡς αὐτοῦ τε καὶ παντὸς τοῦ στρατεύματος ἑπομένου.[27] 32. τοὺς μὲν δὴ ἱππέας ἐδέξαντο οἱ ἀγαθοὶ τῶν Περσῶν· ἐπειδὴ δὲ ἅμα πάντα τὰ δεινὰ παρῆν ἐπ' αὐτούς, ἐνέκλιναν, καὶ οἱ μὲν αὐτῶν[21] εὐθὺς ἐν τῷ ποταμῷ ἔπεσον, οἱ δὲ ἄλλοι ἔφευγον. οἱ δὲ Ἕλληνες ἑπόμενοι αἱροῦσι καὶ τὸ στρατόπεδον αὐτῶν. καὶ οἱ μὲν πελτασταὶ ὥσπερ εἰκὸς ἐφ' ἁρπαγὴν ἐτρέποντο.[32] ὁ δὲ Ἀγησίλαος ἔχων κύκλῳ πάντα καὶ φίλια καὶ πολέμια περιεστρατοπεδεύσατο. 33. ὡς δὲ ἤκουσε τοὺς πολεμίους ταράττεσθαι διὰ τὸ αἰτιᾶσθαι ἀλλήλους τοῦ γεγενημένου,[26b] εὐθὺς ἦγεν ἐπὶ Σάρδεις.

12

He gives liberty to the Asiatic Greeks.

Κἀκεῖ ἅμα μὲν ἔκαιε καὶ ἐπόρθει τὰ περὶ τὸ ἄστυ,[8a] ἅμα δὲ καὶ κηρύγματι[19a] ἐδήλου τοὺς μὲν ἐλευθερίας[26a] δεομένους ὡς πρὸς σύμμαχον αὐτὸν παρεῖναι·[44] εἰ δέ τινες τὴν Ἀσίαν ἑαυτῶν[21] ποιοῦνται, πρὸς τοὺς ἐλευθεροῦντας διακρινουμένους ἐν ὅπλοις παρεῖναι. 34. ἐπεὶ μέντοι οὐδεὶς ἀντεξῄει, ἀδεῶς δὴ τὸ ἀπὸ τούτου[14a] ἐστρατεύετο, τοὺς μὲν πρόσθεν προσκυνεῖν Ἕλληνας ἀναγκαζομένους ὁρῶν τιμωμένους ὑφ' ὧν ὑβρίζοντο, τοὺς δ' ἀξιοῦντας καὶ τὰς τῶν θεῶν τιμὰς καρποῦσθαι,[29a] τούτους ποιήσας μηδ' ἀντιβλέπειν[29d] τοῖς Ἕλλησι δύνασθαι, καὶ τὴν μὲν τῶν φίλων χώραν ἀδῄωτον[12] παρέχων, τὴν δὲ τῶν πολεμίων οὕτω καρπούμενος ὥστε ἐν δυοῖν ἐτοῖν πλέον τῶν ἑκατὸν ταλάντων[25] τῷ θεῷ ἐν Δελφοῖς δεκάτην ἀποθῦσαι.

Execution of Tissaphernes. Effect of Agesilaus' conciliatory policy. His patriotism.

35. Ὁ μέντοι Περσῶν βασιλεύς, νομίσας Τισσαφέρνην αἴτιον εἶναι τοῦ κακῶς φέρεσθαι[21] τὰ ἑαυτοῦ, Τιθραύστην καταπέμψας ἀπέτεμεν αὐτοῦ τὴν κεφαλήν. μετὰ δὲ τοῦτο τὰ μὲν τῶν βαρβάρων ἔτι ἀθυμότερα ἐγένετο,[1a] τὰ δὲ Ἀγησιλάου πολὺ ἐρρωμενέστερα. ἀπὸ πάντων γὰρ τῶν ἐθνῶν ἐπρεσβεύοντο περὶ φιλίας, πολλοὶ δὲ καὶ ἀφίσταντο πρὸς αὐτόν, ὀρεγόμενοι τῆς ἐλευθερίας,[23] ὥστε οὐκέτι Ἑλλήνων[25] μόνον ἀλλὰ καὶ βαρβάρων πολλῶν ἡγεμὼν ἦν[49a] ὁ Ἀγησίλαος.

36. Ἄξιόν γε μὴν καὶ ἐντεῦθεν ὑπερβαλλόντως ἄγασθαι αὐτοῦ,[23] ὅστις ἄρχων μὲν παμπόλλων[25] ἐν τῇ ἠπείρῳ πόλεων, ἄρχων δὲ καὶ νήσων, ἐπεὶ καὶ τὸ ναυτικὸν προσῆψεν αὐτῷ[16] ἡ πόλις, αὐξανόμενος δὲ καὶ εὐκλείᾳ καὶ δυνάμει, παρὸν[61] δ' αὐτῷ πολλοῖς καὶ ἀγαθοῖς[19a] χρῆσθαι ὅ,τι[13] ἐβούλετο, πρὸς δὲ τούτοις τὸ μέγιστον,

ἐπινοῶν καὶ ἐλπίζων καταλύσειν⁴³ᵃ τὴν ἐπὶ τὴν Ἑλλάδα
στρατεύσασαν πρότερον ἀρχήν,⁸ ὅμως ὑπ'⁴¹ᵃ οὐδενὸς
τούτων ἐκρατήθη, ἀλλ' ἐπειδὴ ἦλθεν αὐτῷ ἀπὸ τῶν οἴκοι
τελῶν⁸ βοηθεῖν τῇ πατρίδι, ἐπείθετο τῇ πόλει οὐδὲν δια-
φερόντως ἢ εἰ ἐν τῷ ἐφορείῳ ἔτυχεν⁵⁴ᵇ ἑστηκὼς μόνος
παρὰ τοὺς πέντε, μάλα ἔνδηλον ποιῶν ὡς οὔτε ἂν πᾶσαν
τὴν γῆν δέξαιτο⁶⁷ᵃ ἀντὶ τῆς πατρίδος οὔτε τοὺς ἐπικτήτους
ἀντὶ τῶν ἀρχαίων φίλων οὔτε αἰσχρὰ καὶ ἀκίνδυνα κέρδη
μᾶλλον ἢ μετὰ κινδύνων τὰ καλὰ καὶ δίκαια. 37. ὅσον
γε μὴν χρόνον¹⁴ᵃ ἐπὶ τῇ ἀρχῇ ἔμεινε πῶς οὐκ ἀξιεπαίνου
βασιλέως καὶ τοῦτ' ἔργον ἐπεδείξατο, ὅστις⁵¹ παραλαβὼν
πάσας πόλεις ἐφ' ἃς ἄρξων ἐξέπλευσε στασιαζούσας διὰ
τὸ τὰς πολιτείας κινηθῆναι,³⁰ ἐπεὶ Ἀθηναῖοι τῆς ἀρχῆς²⁴
ἔληξαν, ἐποίησεν ὥστ' ἄνευ φυγῆς καὶ θανάτων ἕως αὐτὸς
παρῆν⁵²ᶜ ὁμονόως πολιτευομένας καὶ εὐδαίμονας τὰς⁵
πόλεις διατελέσαι; 38. τοιγαροῦν οἱ ἐν τῇ Ἀσίᾳ
Ἕλληνες οὐχ ὡς ἄρχοντος μόνον ἀλλὰ καὶ ὡς πατρὸς καὶ
ἑταίρου ἀπιόντος αὐτοῦ²⁷ ἐλυποῦντο. καὶ τέλος ἐδήλωσαν
ὅτι οὐ πλαστὴν⁵ᵃ τὴν φιλίαν παρείχοντο. ἐθελούσιοι γοῦν
αὐτῷ συνεβοήθησαν τῇ Λακεδαίμονι, καὶ ταῦτα εἰδότες
ὅτι οὐ χείροσιν¹⁶ ἑαυτῶν δεήσοι μάχεσθαι. τῶν μὲν δὴ
ἐν τῇ Ἀσίᾳ πράξεων⁸ τοῦτο τέλος ἐγένετο.

CHAPTER II.

AGESILAUS IN EUROPE.

The homeward march; he is attacked by the Thessalians.

1. Διαβὰς⁵⁸ᵇ δὲ τὸν Ἑλλήσποντον ἐπορεύετο διὰ τῶν
αὐτῶν ἐθνῶν ὧνπερ ὁ Πέρσης τῷ παμπληθεῖ στόλῳ· καὶ
ἣν ἐνιαυσίαν ὁδὸν ὁ βάρβαρος ἐποιήσατο, ταύτην μεῖον ἢ

ἐν μηνὶ κατήνυσεν ὁ Ἀγησίλαος. οὐ γὰρ ὡς ὑστερήσειε
τῆς πατρίδος²⁵ προεθυμεῖτο. 2. ἐπεὶ δὲ ἐξαμείψας Μακε-
δονίαν εἰς Θετταλίαν ἀφίκετο,⁵² Λαρισαῖοι μὲν καὶ Κραν-
νώνιοι καὶ Σκοτουσσαῖοι καὶ Φαρσάλιοι σύμμαχοι ὄντες
Βοιωτοῖς,¹⁶ καὶ πάντες δὲ Θετταλοὶ πλὴν ὅσοι αὐτῶν
φυγάδες τότε ὄντες⁵⁹ ἐτύγχανον, ἐκακούργουν οὗτοι ἐφε-
πόμενοι. ὁ δὲ τέως μὲν ἦγεν ἐν πλαισίῳ τὸ στράτευμα,
τοὺς ἡμίσεις μὲν ἔμπροσθεν, τοὺς ἡμίσεις δὲ ἐπ' οὐρὰν
ἔχων τῶν ἱππέων· ἐπεὶ δ' ἐκώλυον τῆς πορείας²⁴ αὐτὸν οἱ
Θετταλοὶ ἐπιτιθέμενοι τοῖς ὄπισθεν,¹⁵ παραπέμπει ἐπ'
οὐρὰν καὶ τὸ ἀπὸ τοῦ προηγουμένου στρατεύματος
ἱππικὸν⁸ πλὴν τῶν⁶⁷ᵃ περὶ αὐτόν. 3. ὡς δὲ παρετάξαντο
ἀλλήλοις,¹⁵ οἱ μὲν Θετταλοί, νομίσαντες οὐκ ἐν καλῷ
εἶναι πρὸς τοὺς ὁπλίτας ἱππομαχεῖν,²⁹ᶜ στρέψαντες
βάδην ἀπεχώρουν· οἱ δὲ μάλα σωφρόνως ἐφείποντο.

*Agesilaus sees his advantage, and by a brisk charge puts them to
flight. His delight at beating the best cavalry in Greece.*

Γνοὺς δὲ ὁ ⁵Ἀγησίλαος ἃ¹³ ἑκάτεροι ἡμάρτανον παραπέμπει τοὺς ἀμφ' αὐτὸν μάλ' εὐρώστους ἱππέας,⁸ καὶ
κελεύει τοῖς τε ἄλλοις παραγγέλλειν⁴⁴ καὶ αὐτοὺς διώκειν
κατὰ κράτος καὶ μηκέτι⁶²ᵃ δοῦναι αὐτοῖς ἀναστροφήν.
οἱ δὲ Θετταλοὶ ὡς εἶδον παρὰ δόξαν ἐλαύνοντας,⁴³ᶜ οἱ μὲν
αὐτῶν οὐδ' ἀνέστρεψαν, οἱ δὲ καὶ ἀναστρέφειν²⁹ᶜ πειρώ-
μενοι πλαγίους⁵ ἔχοντες τοὺς ἵππους ἡλίσκοντο. 4. Πολύ-
χαρμος μέντοι ὁ Φαρσάλιος ἱππαρχῶν ἀνέστρεψέ τε καὶ
μαχόμενος σὺν τοῖς ἀμφ' αὐτὸν⁸ᵃ ἀποθνήσκει. ὡς δὲ
τοῦτο ἐγένετο, φυγὴ γίγνεται ἐξαισία· ὥσθ' οἱ μὲν ἀπέ-
θνησκον⁴⁹ᵃ αὐτῶν, οἱ δὲ καὶ ζῶντες ἡλίσκοντο. ἔστησαν δ'
οὖν οὐ πρόσθεν πρὶν ἐπὶ τῷ ὄρει τῷ Ναρθακίῳ ἐγένοντο.⁵²ᵃ
5. καὶ τότε μὲν δὴ ὁ Ἀγησίλαος τρόπαιόν τε ἐστήσατο
μεταξὺ Πράντος καὶ Ναρθακίου· καὶ αὐτοῦ κατέμεινε,

μάλα ἡδόμενος τῷ ἔργῳ,[19a] ὅτι τοὺς μέγιστον φρονοῦντας
ἐφ᾿ ἱππικῇ ἐνενικήκει σὺν ᾧ[4a] αὐτὸς ἐμηχανήσατο ἱππικῷ.
τῇ δ᾿ ὑστεραίᾳ[19c] ὑπερβάλλων τὰ Ἀχαϊκὰ τῆς Φθίας ὄρη
τὴν λοιπὴν ἤδη πᾶσαν[13] διὰ φιλίας ἐπορεύθη εἰς τὰ Βοιωτῶν ὅρια.

How he prepared for the battle of Coronea.

6. Ἐνταῦθα δὴ ἀντιτεταγμένους εὑρὼν Θηβαίους,
Ἀθηναίους, Ἀργείους, Κορινθίους, Αἰνιᾶνας, Εὐβοέας καὶ
Λοκροὺς ἀμφοτέρους, οὐδὲν ἐμέλλησεν, ἀλλ᾿ ἐκ τοῦ
φανεροῦ[8a] ἀντιπαρέτατττε, Λακεδαιμονίων μὲν ἔχων μόραν
καὶ ἥμισυ, τῶν δ᾿ αὐτόθεν συμμάχων Φωκέας καὶ Ὀρχομενίους μόνους, τό τ᾿ ἄλλο στράτευμα ὅπερ ἡγάγετο αὐτός.
7. καὶ οὐ τοῦτο λέξων[50a] ἔρχομαι ὡς πολὺ μὲν ἐλάττους
πολὺ δὲ χείρονας ἔχων ὅμως συνέβαλεν· εἰ γὰρ ταῦτα
λέγοιμι,[53c] Ἀγησίλαόν τ᾿ ἄν μοι δοκῶ ἄφρονα ἀποφαίνειν[55]
καὶ ἐμαυτὸν μωρόν, εἰ ἐπαινοίην τὸν περὶ τῶν μεγίστων
εἰκῇ κινδυνεύοντα· ἀλλὰ μᾶλλον τάδ᾿ αὐτοῦ ἄγαμαι ὅτι
πλῆθός τε οὐδὲν μεῖον ἢ τὸ τῶν πολεμίων[8a] παρεσκευά-
σατο, ὥπλισέ τε οὕτως ὡς ἅπαντα μὲν χαλκόν, ἅπαντα
δὲ φοινικὰ φαίνεσθαι· 8. ἐπεμελήθη δ᾿ ὅπως οἱ στρατιῶται τοὺς πόνους δυνήσοιντο[50e] ὑποφέρειν· ἐνέπλησε δὲ καὶ
φρονήματος[26a] τὰς ψυχὰς αὐτῶν, ὡς ἱκανοὶ εἶεν[50] πρὸς
οὕστινας δέοι μάχεσθαι· ἔτι δὲ φιλονεικίαν ἐνέβαλε πρὸς
ἀλλήλους τοῖς[16] μετ᾿ αὐτοῦ ὅπως ἕκαστοι αὐτῶν ἄριστοι
φαίνοιντο. ἐλπίδων γε μὴν πάντας ἐνέπλησεν ὡς πᾶσι
πολλὰ κἀγαθὰ ἔσοιτο,[43b] εἰ ἄνδρες ἀγαθοὶ γίγνοιντο, νομίζων ἐκ τῶν τοιούτων ἀνθρώπους προθυμότατα τοῖς
πολεμίοις μάχεσθαι. 9. καὶ μέντοι οὐκ ἐψεύσθη.

Battle of Coronea; the first engagement.

Διηγήσομαι δὲ καὶ τὴν μάχην· καὶ γὰρ ἐγένετο οἵαπερ[48]
οὐκ ἄλλη τῶν ἐφ᾿ ἡμῶν. συνῇεσαν μὲν γὰρ εἰς τὸ κατὰ

16

Κορώνειαν πεδίον[8] οἱ μὲν σὺν Ἀγησιλάῳ[8a] ἀπὸ τοῦ Κηφισοῦ, οἱ δὲ σὺν τοῖς Θηβαίοις ἀπὸ τοῦ Ἑλικῶνος. ἑώρων δὲ τάς τε φάλαγγας ἀλλήλων μάλα ἰσομάχους, σχεδὸν δὲ καὶ οἱ ἱππεῖς ἦσαν ἑκατέρων ἰσοπληθεῖς. εἶχε δὲ ὁ Ἀγησίλαος μὲν τὸ δεξιὸν τοῦ μεθ᾽ ἑαυτοῦ, Ὀρχομένιοι δὲ ἔσχατοι ἦσαν αὐτῷ[17] τοῦ εὐωνύμου. οἱ δ᾽ αὖ Θηβαῖοι αὐτοὶ μὲν δεξιοὶ ἦσαν, Ἀργεῖοι δ᾽ αὐτοῖς τὸ εὐώνυμον εἶχον. 10. συνιόντων[27] δὲ τέως μὲν σιγὴ πολλὴ ἦν ἀπ᾽ ἀμφοτέρων· ἡνίκα δὲ ἀπεῖχον ἀλλήλων[24] ὅσον στάδιον, ἀλαλάξαντες οἱ Θηβαῖοι δρόμῳ[19a] ὁμόσε ἐφέροντο. ὡς δὲ τριῶν ἔτι πλέθρων ἐν μέσῳ ὄντων ἀντεξέδραμον ἀπὸ τῆς Ἀγησιλάου φάλαγγος ὧν[4c] Ἡριππίδας ἐξενάγει. 11. ἦσαν δ᾽ οὗτοι τῶν τε ἐξ οἴκου αὐτῷ συστρατευσαμένων[8a] καὶ τῶν Κυρείων τινές, καὶ Ἴωνες δὲ καὶ Αἰολεῖς καὶ Ἑλλησπόντιοι ἐχόμενοι. καὶ πάντες οὗτοι τῶν συνεκδραμόντων[21a] τε ἐγένοντο καὶ εἰς δόρυ ἀφικόμενοι ἐτρέψαντο τὸ καθ᾽ ἑαυτούς.[8a] Ἀργεῖοι μέντοι οὐκ ἐδέξαντο τοὺς ἀμφ᾽ Ἀγησίλαον, ἀλλ᾽ ἔφυγον ἐπὶ τὸν Ἑλικῶνα.

The battle renewed.   Bravery of Agesilaus.

Κἀνταῦθα οἱ μεν τινες τῶν ξένων ἐστεφάνουν[32] ἤδη τὸν Ἀγησίλαον, ἀγγέλλει δέ τις αὐτῷ ὅτι Θηβαῖοι τοὺς Ὀρχομενίους διακόψαντες ἐν τοῖς σκευοφόροις εἰσί.[43b]   καὶ ὁ μὲν εὐθὺς ἐξελίξας[58i] τὴν φάλαγγα ἦγεν ἐπ᾽ αὐτούς· οἱ δ᾽ αὖ Θηβαῖοι ὡς εἶδον τοὺς συμμάχους πρὸς τῷ Ἑλικῶνι πεφευγότας,[43c] διαπεσεῖν βουλόμενοι πρὸς τοὺς ἑαυτῶν ἐχώρουν ἐρρωμένως· 12. ἐνταῦθα δὴ Ἀγησίλαον ἀνδρεῖον μὲν ἔξεστιν εἰπεῖν ἀναμφιλόγως, οὐ μέντοι εἵλετό γε τὰ ἀσφαλέστατα·[8a] ἐξὸν[61] γὰρ αὐτῷ παρέντι[18] τοὺς διαπίπτοντας ἑπομένῳ χειροῦσθαι τοὺς ὄπισθεν οὐκ ἐποίησε τοῦτο, ἀλλ᾽ ἀντιμέτωπος συνέρραξε τοῖς Θηβαίοις.[16]   καὶ συμβαλόντες τὰς ἀσπίδας ἐωθοῦντο, ἐμάχοντο, ἀπέκτεινον, ἀπέθνησκον.[32] καὶ κραυγὴ μὲν οὐδεμία παρῆν, οὐ μὴν οὐδὲ σιγή, φωνὴ δέ τις ἦν τοιαύτη οἵαν ὀργή τε καὶ μάχη παράσχοιτ' ἄν.[54b] τέλος δὲ τῶν Θηβαίων[21] οἱ μὲν δια- πίπτουσι πρὸς τὸν Ἑλικῶνα, πολλοὶ δ' ἀποχωροῦντες[58b] ἀπέθανον.

His respect for the rights of sanctuary.

13. ἐπειδὴ δὲ ἡ μὲν νίκη σὺν Ἀγησιλάῳ ἐγένετο, τετρωμένος δ' αὐτὸς προσηνέχθη πρὸς τὴν φάλαγγα, προσελάσαντές τινες τῶν ἱππέων λέγουσιν αὐτῷ ὅτι τῶν πολεμίων ὀγδοήκοντα σὺν τοῖς ὅπλοις ὑπὸ τῷ ναῷ εἰσι,[43b] καὶ ἠρώτων τί χρὴ ποιεῖν.[45,47] ὁ δὲ καίπερ πολλὰ τραύματα ἔχων[58d] πάντοσε καὶ παντοίοις ὅπλοις ὅμως οὐκ ἐπελάθετο τοῦ θείου,[23] ἀλλ' ἐᾶν[44] τε ἀπιέναι ὅποι βούλοιντο ἐκέλευε καὶ ἀδικεῖν οὐκ εἴα,[63] καὶ προπέμψαι ἐπέταξε τοὺς ἀμφ' αὐτὸν ἱππεῖς ἔστε ἐν τῷ ἀσφαλεῖ ἐγένοντο.[52]

The battle-field. Defeat of the Thebans.

14. Ἐπεί γε μὴν ἔληξεν ἡ μάχη, παρῆν[29a] δὴ θεά- σασθαι ἔνθα συνέπεσον ἀλλήλοις[16] τὴν μὲν γῆν αἵματι πεφυρμένην,[43c] νεκροὺς δὲ κειμένους φιλίους καὶ πολε- μίους μετ' ἀλλήλων, ἀσπίδας δὲ διατεθρυμμένας, δόρατα συντεθραυσμένα, ἐγχειρίδια γυμνὰ κολεῶν,[24] τὰ μὲν χαμαί, τὰ δ' ἐν σώμασι, τὰ δ' ἔτι μετὰ χεῖρας. 15. τότε μὲν οὖν, καὶ γὰρ ἦν ἤδη ὀψέ, συνελκύσαντες τοὺς τῶν πολε- μίων νεκροὺς εἴσω φάλαγγος[25] ἐδειπνοποιήσαντο καὶ ἐκοιμήθησαν· πρωῒ δὲ Γῦλιν τὸν πολέμαρχον παρα- τάξαι τε ἐκέλευσε τὸ στράτευμα καὶ τρόπαιον ἵστασθαι καὶ στεφανοῦσθαι πάντας τῷ θεῷ[17] καὶ τοὺς αὐλητὰς πάντας αὐλεῖν. 16. καὶ οἱ μὲν ταῦτ' ἐποίουν· οἱ δὲ Θηβαῖοι ἔπεμψαν κήρυκα, ὑποσπόνδους[5] τοὺς νεκροὺς

18

αἰτοῦντες θάψαι. καὶ οὕτω δὴ αἵ τε σπονδαὶ γίγνονται καὶ ὁ Ἀγησίλαος οἴκαδε ἀπεχώρει, ἑλόμενος ἀντὶ τοῦ μέγιστος⁹ εἶναι ἐν τῇ Ἀσίᾳ οἴκοι τὰ νόμιμα¹³ μὲν ἄρχειν, τὰ νόμιμα δὲ ἄρχεσθαι.

The Corinthian campaign. He takes the Long Walls, and by stratagem obtains possession of Peiraeum.

17. Ἐκ δὲ τούτου κατανοήσας τοὺς Ἀργείους τὰ μὲν οἴκοι καρπουμένους,⁴³ᶜ Κόρινθον δὲ προσειληφότας, ἡδομένους δὲ τῷ πολέμῳ¹⁶ στρατεύει ἐπ' αὐτούς. καὶ δῃώσας πᾶσαν αὐτῶν τὴν χώραν εὐθὺς ἐκεῖθεν ὑπερβαλὼν κατὰ τὰ στενὰ εἰς Κόρινθον αἱρεῖ τὰ ἐπὶ τὸ Λέχαιον τείνοντα⁸ τείχη· καὶ ἀναπετάσας τῆς Πελοποννήσου τὰς πύλας οὕτως οἴκαδε ἀπελθὼν εἰς τὰ Ὑακίνθια ὅπου ἐτάχθη ὑπὸ τοῦ χοροποιοῦ τὸν παιᾶνα τῷ θεῷ¹⁶ συνεπετέλει. 18. ἐκ τούτου δὲ αἰσθανόμενος τοὺς Κορινθίους πάντα μὲν τὰ κτήνη ἐν τῷ Πειραίῳ σωζομένους,⁴³ᶜ πᾶν δὲ τὸ Πείραιον σπείροντας καὶ καρπουμένους, μέγιστον δὲ ἡγησάμενος, ὅτι Βοιωτοὶ ταύτῃ ἐκ Κρεύσιος ὁρμώμενοι εὐπετῶς τοῖς Κορινθίοις παρεγίγνοντο,⁵¹ στρατεύει ἐπὶ τὸ Πείραιον. ἰδὼν δὲ ὑπὸ πολλῶν φυλαττόμενον, ὡς ἐνδιδομένης τῆς πόλεως²⁷ ἐξ ἀρίστου μετεστρατοπεδεύσατο πρὸς τὸ ἄστυ· 19. αἰσθόμενος δὲ ὑπὸ νύκτα βεβοηθηκότας⁴³ᶜ ἐκ τοῦ Πειραίου εἰς τὴν πόλιν πασσυδίᾳ, ὑποστρέψας ἅμα τῇ ἡμέρᾳ αἱρεῖ τὸ Πείραιον, ἔρημον εὑρὼν φυλακῆς,²⁴ καὶ τά τε ἄλλα τὰ ἐνόντα λαμβάνει καὶ τὰ τείχη ἃ ἐνετετείχιστο. ταῦτα δὲ ποιήσας⁵⁸ᵇ οἴκαδε ἀπεχώρησε.

Agesilaus as defender of the friends of Sparta. The Theban campaigns.

20. Μετὰ δὲ ταῦτα προθύμων ὄντων τῶν Ἀχαιῶν²⁷ εἰς τὴν συμμαχίαν καὶ δεομένων συστρατεύειν⁴⁴ αὐτοῖς

εἰς Ἀκαρνανίαν, καὶ ἐπιθεμένων ἐν στενοῖς τῶν Ἀκαρνάνων, καταλαβὼν τοῖς ψιλοῖς[19a] τὰ ὑπὲρ κεφαλῆς αὐτῶν
μάχην συνάπτει καὶ πολλοὺς ἀποκτείνας αὐτῶν τρόπαιον
ἐστήσατο, καὶ οὐ πρότερον ἔληξε πρὶν Ἀχαιοῖς μὲν φίλους
ἐποίησεν[52a] Ἀκαρνᾶνας καὶ Αἰτωλοὺς καὶ Ἀργείους,
ἑαυτῷ δὲ καὶ συμμάχους. 21. ἐπειδὴ δὲ εἰρήνης[23] ἐπι-
θυμήσαντες οἱ πολέμιοι ἐπρεσβεύοντο, Ἀγησίλαος ἀντεῖπε
τῇ εἰρήνῃ,[8a] ἕως τοὺς διὰ Λακεδαιμονίους φυγόντας[16] Κορινθίων καὶ Θηβαίων[21] ἠνάγκασε[52] τὰς πόλεις οἴκαδε κατα-
δέξασθαι· ὕστερον δ' αὖ καὶ Φλιασίων τοὺς διὰ Λακεδαιμονίους φυγόντας κατήγαγεν, αὐτὸς στρατευσάμενος[58f]
ἐπὶ Φλιοῦντα. εἰ δέ τις ἄλλῃ πῃ ταῦτα μέμφεται, ἀλλ'
οὖν φιλεταιρίᾳ γε πραχθέντα[59] φανερά ἐστι. 22. καὶ
γὰρ ἐπεὶ τοὺς ἐν Θήβαις τῶν Λακεδαιμονίων κατέκανον
οἱ ἐναντίοι, βοηθῶν αὖ τούτοις[16] στρατεύει ἐπὶ τὰς Θήβας.
εὑρὼν δὲ ἀποτεταφρευμένα καὶ ἀπεσταυρωμένα ἅπαντα,
ὑπερβὰς τὰς Κυνὸς κεφαλὰς ἐδῄου τὴν χώραν μέχρι τοῦ
ἄστεος,[67a] παρέχων καὶ ἐν πεδίῳ καὶ ἀνὰ τὰ ὄρη μάχεσθαι
Θηβαίοις, εἰ βούλοιντο. ἐστράτευσε δὲ καὶ τῷ ἐπιόντι
ἔτει[19c] πάλιν ἐπὶ Θήβας· καὶ ὑπερβὰς τὰ κατὰ Σκῶλον
σταυρώματα καὶ τάφρους ἐδῄωσε τὰ λοιπὰ τῆς Βοιω-
τίας.[20f]

*His services to his country in her extremity. He avenges her
friends, and makes the most of her remaining resources.*

23. Τὰ μὲν δὴ μέχρι τούτου κοινῇ αὐτός τε καὶ ἡ πόλις
εὐτύχει· ὅσα γε μὴν μετὰ τοῦτο σφάλματα ἐγένοντο
οὐδεὶς ἂν εἴποι[54b] ὡς Ἀγησιλάου ἡγουμένου[27] ἐπράχθη.
ἐπεὶ δ' αὖ τῆς ἐν Λεύκτροις συμφορᾶς γεγενημένης κατα-
καίνουσι τοὺς ἐν Τεγέᾳ φίλους καὶ ξένους αὐτοῦ οἱ
ἀντίπαλοι σὺν Μαντινεῦσι, συνεστηκότων ἤδη Βοιωτῶν
τε πάντων[27,58b] καὶ Ἀρκάδων καὶ Ἠλείων, στρατεύει

σὺν μόνῃ τῇ Λακεδαιμονίων δυνάμει, πολλῶν νομιζόντων
οὐδ' ἂν ἐξελθεῖν[55] Λακεδαιμονίους πολλοῦ χρόνου ἐκ τῆς
αὑτῶν. δῃώσας δὲ τὴν χώραν τῶν κατακανόντων τοὺς
φίλους οὕτως αὖ οἴκαδε ἀπεχώρησεν. 24. ἀπό γε μὴν
τούτου ἐπὶ τὴν Λακεδαίμονα στρατευσαμένων[27] Ἀρκάδων
τε πάντων καὶ Ἀργείων καὶ Ἠλείων καὶ Βοιωτῶν, καὶ σὺν
αὐτοῖς Φωκέων καὶ Λοκρῶν ἀμφοτέρων καὶ Θετταλῶν καὶ
Αἰνιάνων καὶ Ἀκαρνάνων καὶ Εὐβοέων, πρὸς δὲ τούτοις
ἀφεστηκότων μὲν τῶν δούλων, πολλῶν δὲ περιοικίδων
πόλεων, καὶ αὐτῶν Σπαρτιατῶν οὐ μειόνων ἀπολωλότων
ἐν τῇ ἐν Λεύκτροις μάχῃ ἢ λειπομένων, ὅμως διεφύλαξε
τὴν πόλιν, καὶ ταῦτα ἀτείχιστον οὖσαν,[58d] ὅπου μὲν τῷ
παντὶ πλεῖον ἂν εἶχον[54b] οἱ πολέμιοι, οὐκ ἐξάγων ἐνταῦθα,
ὅπου δὲ οἱ πολῖται πλέον ἕξειν ἔμελλον, εὐρώστως παρα-
τεταγμένος, νομίζων εἰς μὲν τὸ πλατὺ ἐξιὼν[9,58o] πάντοθεν
ἂν περιέχεσθαι, ἐν δὲ τοῖς στενοῖς καὶ ὑπερδεξίοις τόποις
ὑπομένων τῷ παντὶ[19b] κρατεῖν ἄν.

When past military service, he serves his country in other ways.

25. Ἐπεί γε μὴν ἀπεχώρησε τὸ στράτευμα, πῶς οὐκ
ἂν φαίη τις αὐτὸν εὐγνωμόνως χρῆσθαι ἑαυτῷ; ὡς γὰρ
τοῦ στρατεύεσθαι[24] αὐτὸν καὶ πεζῇ καὶ ἐφ' ἵππων ἀπεῖρ-
γεν ἤδη τὸ γῆρας, χρημάτων[26a] δὲ ἑώρα τὴν πόλιν δεομένην,
εἰ μέλλοι[27a] σύμμαχόν τινα ἕξειν, ἐπὶ τὸ πορίζειν ταῦτα
ἑαυτὸν ἔταξε. καὶ ὅσα μὲν ἐδύνατο οἴκοι μένων ἐμηχανᾶτο, ἃ δὲ καιρὸς ἦν οὐκ ὤκνει μετιέναι, οὐδ' ᾐσχύνετο, εἰ
μέλλοι τὴν πόλιν ὠφελήσειν, πρεσβευτὴς ἐκπορευόμενος[59]
ἀντὶ στρατηγοῦ.

His achievements in diplomacy.

26. ὅμως δὲ καὶ ἐν τῇ πρεσβείᾳ μεγάλου στρατηγοῦ[21]
ἔργα διεπράξατο. Αὐτοφραδάτης τε γὰρ πολιορκῶν ἐν

Ἄσσῳ Ἀριοβαρζάνην σύμμαχον ὄντα δείσας[58a] Ἀγησίλαον
φεύγων ᾤχετο· Κότυς δ᾽ αὖ, Σηστὸν πολιορκῶν Ἀριο-
βαρζάνου[21] ἔτι οὖσαν,[58b] λύσας καὶ οὗτος τὴν πολιορκίαν
ἀπηλλάγη· ὥστ᾽ οὐκ ἀλόγως καὶ ἀπὸ τῆς πρεσβείας
τρόπαιον τῶν πολεμίων ἑστήκει αὐτῷ.[17] / Μαύσωλός γε
μὴν κατὰ θάλατταν ἑκατὸν ναυσὶ πολιορκῶν ἀμφότερα
τὰ χωρία ταῦτα οὐκέτι δείσας ἀλλὰ πεισθεὶς[58a] ἀπέπλευ-
σεν οἴκαδε. 27. κἀνταῦθα οὖν ἄξια θαύματος[25a] διεπρά-
ξατο· οἵ τε γὰρ εὖ πεπονθέναι νομίζοντες ὑπ᾽ αὐτοῦ καὶ
οἱ φεύγοντες αὐτὸν χρήματα, ἀμφότεροι ἔδοσαν. Ταχώς
γε μὴν καὶ Μαύσωλος, διὰ τὴν πρόσθεν Ἀγησιλάου
ξενίαν συμβαλόμενος[41b] καὶ οὗτος χρήματα τῇ Λακεδαίμονι, ἀπέπεμψαν αὐτὸν οἴκαδε προπομπὴν δόντες μεγα-
λοπρεπῆ.

His last campaign in Egypt. The Egyptians throw off their king,
and the monarchy is divided. Agesilaus' choice between them.

28. Ἐκ δὲ τούτου ἤδη μὲν ἐγεγόνει ἔτη[14a] ἀμφὶ τὰ
ὀγδοήκοντα· κατανενοηκὼς δὲ τὸν Αἰγυπτίων βασιλέα
ἐπιθυμοῦντα[43c] τῷ Πέρσῃ πολεμεῖν,[29c] καὶ πολλοὺς μὲν
πεζούς, πολλοὺς δὲ ἱππέας, πολλὰ δὲ χρήματα ἔχοντα,
ἄσμενος ἤκουσεν ὅτι μετεπέμπετο αὐτόν, καὶ ταῦτα
ἡγεμονίαν ὑπισχνούμενος. 29. ἐνόμιζε γὰρ τῇ αὐτῇ
ὁρμῇ[19] τῷ μὲν Αἰγυπτίῳ χάριν ἀποδώσειν ἀνθ᾽ ὧν[4a] εὐερ-
γετήκει τὴν Λακεδαίμονα, τοὺς δ᾽ ἐν τῇ Ἀσίᾳ Ἕλληνας[8]
πάλιν ἐλευθερώσειν, τῷ δὲ Πέρσῃ[16] δίκην ἐπιθήσειν καὶ
τῶν πρόσθεν[26b] καὶ ὅτι νῦν σύμμαχος[9] εἶναι φάσκων
ἐπέταττε Μεσσήνην ἀφιέναι. 30. ἐπεὶ μέντοι ὁ μετα-
πεμψάμενος οὐκ ἀπεδίδου τὴν ἡγεμονίαν αὐτῷ, ὁ μὲν Ἀγησίλαος ὡς τὸ μέγιστον ἐξηπατημένος ἐφρόντιζε τί δεῖ[47]
ποιεῖν. ἐκ τούτου δὲ πρῶτον μὲν οἱ δίχα στρατευόμενοί τῶν
Αἰγυπτίων ἀφίστανται τοῦ βασιλέως,[24] ἔπειτα δὲ καὶ οἱ

22

ἄλλοι πάντες ἀπέλιπον αὐτόν. καὶ αὐτὸς μὲν δείσας ἀπεχώρησε φυγῇ[19a] εἰς Σιδῶνα τῆς Φοινίκης,[21] οἱ δ' Αἰγύπτιοι στασιάζοντες διττοὺς βασιλέας αἱροῦνται.[41b] 31. ἐνταῦθα δὴ 'Αγησίλαος γνοὺς ὅτι εἰ μὲν μηδετέρῳ[16] συλλήψοιτο, μισθὸν οὐδέτερος λύσει τοῖς "Ελλησιν, ἀγορὰν δὲ οὐδέτερος παρέξει, ὁπότερός τ' ἂν κρατήσῃ,[43] οὗτος ἐχθρὸς ἔσται· εἰ δὲ τῷ ἑτέρῳ συλλήψοιτο, οὗτός γε εὖ παθὼν ὡς τὸ εἰκὸς φίλος ἔσοιτο,[43b] οὕτω δὴ κρίνας, ὁπότερος φιλέλλην μᾶλλον ἐδόκει εἶναι, στρατευσάμενος μετὰ τούτου τὸν μὲν μισέλληνα μάχῃ νικήσας χειροῦται, τὸν δ' ἕτερον συγκαθίστησιν· καὶ φίλον ποιήσας τῇ Λακεδαίμονι καὶ χρήματα πολλὰ προσλαβὼν οὕτως ἀποπλεῖ οἴκαδε καίπερ μέσου χειμῶνος ὄντος,[58d,27] σπεύδων ὡς μὴ ἀργὸς ἡ πόλις εἰς τὸ ἐπιὸν θέρος πρὸς τοὺς πολεμίους γένοιτο.[50e,37a]

CHAPTER III.

Agesilaus' religious observance of good faith.

1. Καὶ ταῦτα μὲν δὴ εἴρηται ὅσα τῶν ἐκείνου ἔργων[21a] μετὰ πλείστων μαρτύρων ἐπράχθη. τὰ γὰρ τοιαῦτα οὐ τεκμηρίων[26a] προσδεῖται, ἀλλ' ἀναμνῆσαι[29a] μόνον ἀρκεῖ καὶ εὐθὺς πιστεύεται. νῦν δὲ τὴν ἐν τῇ ψυχῇ αὐτοῦ ἀρετὴν πειράσομαι δηλοῦν, δι' ἥν ταῦτα ἔπραττε καὶ πάντων τῶν καλῶν[23] ἤρα καὶ πάντα τὰ αἰσχρὰ ἐξεδίωκεν. 2. 'Αγησίλαος γὰρ τὰ μὲν θεῖα οὕτως ἐσέβετο ὡς[49Obs.] καὶ οἱ πολέμιοι τοὺς ἐκείνου ὅρκους καὶ τὰς ἐκείνου σπονδὰς πιστοτέρας ἐνόμιζον ἢ τὴν ἑαυτῶν φιλίαν· οἳ μὲν ὤκνουν εἰς ταὐτὸν ἰέναι, 'Αγησιλάῳ δὲ αὐτοὺς ἐνεχείριζον. ὅπως δὲ μή τις ἀπιστῇ,[50] καὶ ὀνομάσαι βούλομαι τοὺς ἐπιφανεστάτους αὐτῶν.[21a]

23

*Examples of the confidence that it won for him.   Instances
of its success.*

3. Σπιθριδάτης μέν γε ὁ Πέρσης εἰδὼς ὅτι Φαρνάβαζος γῆμαι μὲν τὴν βασιλέως ἔπραττε[43b] θυγατέρα, τὴν δ᾽ αὐτοῦ ἄνευ γάμου λαβεῖν ἐβούλετο, ὕβριν νομίσας τοῦτο Ἀγησιλάῳ ἑαυτὸν καὶ τὴν γυναῖκα καὶ τὰ τέκνα καὶ τὴν δύναμιν ἐνεχείρισε.   4. Κότυς δὲ ὁ τῶν Παφλαγόνων[25] ἄρχων βασιλεῖ μὲν οὐχ ὑπήκουσε[16] δεξιὰν πέμποντι,[58d] φοβούμενος μὴ ληφθεὶς ἢ χρήματα πολλὰ ἀποτίσειεν[43d] ἢ καὶ ἀποθάνοι, Ἀγησιλάου δὲ καὶ οὗτος ταῖς σπονδαῖς πιστεύσας εἰς τὸ στρατόπεδόν τε ἦλθε καὶ συμμαχίαν ποιησάμενος[41b] εἵλετο σὺν Ἀγησιλάῳ στρατεύεσθαι,[29a] χιλίους μὲν ἱππέας, δισχιλίους δὲ πελτοφόρους ἔχων. 5. ἀφίκετο δὲ καὶ Φαρνάβαζος Ἀγησιλάῳ[15] εἰς λόγους καὶ διωμολόγησεν, εἰ μὴ αὐτὸς πάσης τῆς στρατιᾶς στρατηγὸς κατασταθείη, ἀποστήσεσθαι[55] βασιλέως· ἢν μέντοι ἐγὼ γένωμαι στρατηγός, ἔφη, πολεμήσω[53b] σοι, ὦ Ἀγησίλαε, ὡς ἂν ἐγὼ δύνωμαι κράτιστα.[57]   καὶ ταῦτα λέγων ἐπίστευε μηδὲν[62] ἂν παράσπονδον παθεῖν.   οὕτω μέγα καὶ καλὸν κτῆμα τοῖς τε ἄλλοις ἅπασι καὶ ἀνδρὶ δὴ στρατηγῷ τὸ ὅσιόν τε καὶ πιστὸν[9] εἶναί τε καὶ ὄντα[43c] ἐγνῶσθαι.   καὶ περὶ μὲν εὐσεβείας ταῦτα.

CHAPTER IV.

His uprightness and strict honesty, (1) *in private relations;*

1. Περί γε μὴν τῆς εἰς χρήματα δικαιοσύνης[8] ποῖα ἄν τις μείζω τεκμήρια ἔχοι[54b] τῶνδε ; ὑπὸ γὰρ Ἀγησιλάου στέρεσθαι[29a] μὲν οὐδεὶς οὐδὲν πώποτε ἐνεκάλεσεν, εὖ δὲ πεπονθέναι[1] πολλοὶ πολλὰ[13] ὡμολόγουν. ὅτῳ δὲ ἡδὺ τὰ

24

αὐτοῦ διδόναι ἐπ' ὠφελείᾳ ἀνθρώπων, πῶς ἂν οὗτος ἐθέλοι τὰ ἀλλότρια ἀποστερεῖν ἐφ' ᾧ κακόδοξος⁹ εἶναι; εἰ γὰρ χρημάτων²³ ἐπιθυμοίη, πολὺ ἀπραγμονέστερον τὰ αὐτοῦ φυλάττειν ἢ τὰ μὴ⁶²ᵇ προσήκοντα λαμβάνειν. 2. ὃς δὲ δὴ καὶ χάριτας ἀποστερεῖν μὴ ἐθέλοι,⁴⁰ᵇ ὧν οὐκ εἰσὶ δίκαι πρὸς τὸν μὴ ἀποδιδόντα, πῶς ἅ γε καὶ νόμος κωλύει ἐθέλοι ἂν ἀποστερεῖν; Ἀγησίλαος δὲ οὐ μόνον τὸ μὴ⁶²ᵇ ἀποδιδόναι χάριτας ἄδικον ἔκρινεν, ἀλλὰ καὶ τὸ μὴ πολὺ μείζους τὸν μείζω δυνάμενον.

(2) *in the administration of public funds.*

3. Τά γε μὴν τῆς πόλεως⁸ κλέπτειν²⁹ᵃ πῇ ἄν τις αὐτὸν εἰκότως αἰτιάσαιτο, ὃς καὶ τὰς αὐτῷ χάριτας ὀφειλομένας τῇ πατρίδι καρποῦσθαι παρεδίδου; τὸ δ' ὁπότε βούλοιτο εὖ ποιεῖν ἢ πόλιν ἢ φίλους χρήμασι, δύνασθαι παρ' ἑτέρων λαμβάνοντα ὠφελεῖν, οὐ καὶ τοῦτο μέγα τεκμήριον ἐγκρατείας χρημάτων; 4. εἰ γὰρ ἐπώλει τὰς χάριτας ἢ μισθοῦ²⁵ᵃ εὐεργέτει, οὐδεὶς ἂν οὐδὲν ὀφείλειν αὐτῷ ἐνόμισεν·⁵³ᵈ,⁵⁴ᵇ ἀλλ' οἱ προῖκα εὖ πεπονθότες,⁸ᵃ οὗτοι ἀεὶ ἡδέως ὑπηρετοῦσι τῷ εὐεργέτῃ, καὶ διότι εὖ ἔπαθον καὶ διότι προεπιστεύθησαν ἄξιοι εἶναι παρακαταθήκην χάριτος φυλάττειν.

He was not only just, but liberal.

5. Ὅστις δ' ᾑρεῖτο καὶ σὺν τῷ γενναίῳ μειονεκτεῖν ἢ σὺν τῷ ἀδίκῳ πλέον ἔχειν, πῶς οὗτος οὐκ ἂν πολὺ τὴν αἰσχροκέρδειαν ἀποφεύγοι; ⁵⁴ᵇ ἐκεῖνος τοίνυν κριθεὶς ὑπὸ τῆς πόλεως⁴¹ᵃ ἅπαντα ἔχειν τὰ Ἄγιδος τὰ ἡμίσεα⁵⁶ τοῖς ἀπὸ μητρὸς αὐτῷ ὁμογόνοις μετέδωκεν, ὅτι πενομένους αὐτοὺς ἑώρα. ὡς δὲ ταῦτα ἀληθῆ πᾶσα μάρτυς ἡ τῶν Λακεδαιμονίων πόλις. 6. διδόντος δ' αὐτῷ πάμπολλα

c   25

δῶρα Τιθραύστου,[27] εἰ ἀπέλθοι[53] ἐκ τῆς χώρας, ἀπεκρίνατο
ὁ Ἀγησίλαος, Ὦ Τιθραύστα, νομίζεται παρ᾽ ἡμῖν τῷ
ἄρχοντι κάλλιον εἶναι τὴν στρατιὰν ἢ ἑαυτὸν πλουτίζειν,
καὶ παρὰ τῶν πολεμίων λάφυρα μᾶλλον πειρᾶσθαι ἢ
δῶρα λαμβάνειν.

CHAPTER V.

*His temperance, and readiness to bear hardships.   He gave up his
privileges as a commander, to share the labour and the fare of
the private soldier.*

1. Ἀλλὰ μὴν καὶ ὅσαι γε ἡδοναὶ πολλῶν[26] κρατοῦσιν
ἀνθρώπων, ποίας οἶδέ τις Ἀγησίλαον ἡττηθέντα;[43c] ὃς
μέθης[24] μὲν ἀποσχέσθαι ὁμοίως ᾤετο χρῆναι καὶ μανίας,
σίτων δ᾽ ὑπὲρ καιρὸν ὁμοίως καὶ ἀργίας. διμοιρίαν γε
μὴν λαμβάνων[58b] ἐν ταῖς θοίναις οὐχ ὅπως ἀμφοτέραις[19a]
ἐχρῆτο, ἀλλὰ διαπέμπων οὐδετέραν αὑτῷ κατέλειπε,
νομίζων βασιλεῖ τοῦτο διπλασιασθῆναι οὐχὶ πλησμονῆς
ἕνεκα,[57a] ἀλλ᾽ ὅπως ἔχοι[50] καὶ τούτῳ τιμᾶν εἴ τινα βούλοιτο.
2. οὐ μὴν ὕπνῳ γε δεσπότῃ ἀλλ᾽ ἀρχομένῳ ὑπὸ τῶν
πράξεων ἐχρῆτο, καὶ εὐνήν γε εἰ μὴ τῶν συνόντων[21a]
φαυλοτάτην ἔχοι, αἰδούμενος[59] οὐκ ἄδηλος ἦν· ἡγεῖτο γὰρ
ἄρχοντι προσήκειν οὐ μαλακίᾳ[19a] ἀλλὰ καρτερίᾳ τῶν ἰδιωτῶν περιεῖναι. 3. τάδε μέντοι πλεονεκτῶν οὐκ ᾐσχύνετο,
ἐν μὲν τῷ θέρει τοῦ ἡλίου,[21a] ἐν δὲ τῷ χειμῶνι τοῦ ψύχους·
καὶ μὴν εἴ ποτε μοχθῆσαι στρατιᾷ συμβαίη,[40b] ἑκὼν
ἐπόνει παρὰ τοὺς ἄλλους, νομίζων πάντα τὰ τοιαῦτα
παραμυθίαν εἶναι τοῖς στρατιώταις. ὡς δὲ συνελόντι
εἰπεῖν,[29e] Ἀγησίλαος πονῶν[59] μὲν ἠγάλλετο, ῥᾳστώνην δὲ
πάμπαν οὐ προσίετο.

26

CHAPTER VI.

His bravery. His victories were not stolen by chance, but
fairly won in hard-fought fight.

1. Ἀνδρείας γε μὴν οὐκ ἀφανῆ τεκμήριά μοι δοκεῖ
παρασχέσθαι ὑφιστάμενος⁵⁸¹ μὲν ἀεὶ πολεμεῖν πρὸς τοὺς
ἰσχυροτάτους τῶν ἐχθρῶν²¹ᵃ τῇ τε πόλει καὶ τῇ Ἑλλάδι,
ἐν δὲ τοῖς πρὸς τούτους ἀγῶσι⁹ πρῶτον ἑαυτὸν τάττων.
2. ἔνθα γε μὴν ἠθέλησαν αὐτῷ οἱ πολέμιοι μάχην συνάψαι,
οὐ φόβῳ τρεψάμενος νίκης²³ ἔτυχεν, ἀλλὰ μάχῃ ἀντι-
τύπῳ¹⁹ᵃ κρατήσας τρόπαιον ἐστήσατο, ἀθάνατα μὲν τῆς
ἑαυτοῦ ἀρετῆς μνημεῖα καταλιπών, σαφῆ δὲ καὶ αὐτὸς
σημεῖα ἀπενεγκάμενος⁴¹ᵇ τοῦ θυμῷ μάχεσθαι·³⁰ ὥστ’ οὐκ
ἀκούοντας ἀλλ’ ὁρῶντας ἐξῆν¹⁹ᵃ αὐτοῦ τὴν ψυχὴν δοκι-
μάζειν. 3. τρόπαια μὴν Ἀγησιλάου οὐχ ὅσα ἐστήσατο
ἀλλ’ ὅσα¹³ ἐστρατεύσατο δίκαιον νομίζειν. μεῖον μὲν γὰρ
οὐδὲν ἐκράτει ὅτε οὐκ ἤθελον αὐτῷ¹⁶ οἱ πολέμιοι μάχεσθαι,
ἀκινδυνότερον δὲ καὶ συμφορώτερον τῇ τε πόλει καὶ τοῖς
συμμάχοις· καὶ ἐν τοῖς ἀγῶσι δὲ οὐδὲν ἧττον τοὺς ἀκονιτὶ
ἢ τοὺς διὰ μάχης νικῶντας⁸ᵃ στεφανοῦσι.

He won the obedience of his men by winning their love.

4. Τήν γε μὴν σοφίαν αὐτοῦ ποῖαι τῶν ἐκείνου πράξεων
οὐκ ἐπιδεικνύουσιν; ὃς τῇ μὲν πατρίδι οὕτως ἐχρῆτο ὥστε
μάλιστα πειθόμενος [αὐτῇ ποιεῖν ὃ βούλοιτο], ἑταίροις¹⁶
δὲ πρόθυμος ὢν ἀπροφασίστους τοὺς φίλους ἐκέκτητο·
τοὺς δέ γε στρατιώτας ἅμα πειθομένους καὶ φιλοῦντας
αὐτὸν παρεῖχε. καίτοι πῶς ἂν ἰσχυροτέρα γένοιτο φάλαγξ
ἢ διὰ τὸ μὲν πείθεσθαι εὔτακτος οὖσα,⁵⁸ᶜ διὰ δὲ τὸ φιλεῖν
τὸν ἄρχοντα πιστῶς παροῦσα;

His bravery was combined with skilful strategy,

5. Τούς γε μὴν πολεμίους εἶχε ψέγειν μὲν οὐ δυνα-
μένους,[5] μισεῖν δὲ ἀναγκαζομένους. τοὺς γὰρ συμμάχους
ἀεὶ πλέον ἔχειν αὐτῶν[20] ἐμηχανᾶτο, ἐξαπατῶν μὲν ὅπου
καιρὸς εἴη,[40b] φθάνων δὲ ὅπου τάχους δέοι, λήθων δὲ ὅπου
τοῦτο συμφέροι, πάντα δὲ τἀναντία πρὸς τοὺς πολεμίους
ἢ πρὸς τοὺς φίλους ἐπιτηδεύων. 6. καὶ γὰρ νυκτὶ μὲν
ὅσαπερ[13] ἡμέρᾳ ἐχρῆτο, ἡμέρᾳ δὲ ὅσαπερ νυκτί, πολλάκις
ἄδηλος γιγνόμενος ὅπου τε εἴη[45] καὶ ὅποι ἴοι καὶ ὅ,τι
ποιήσοι. ὥστε καὶ τὰ ἐχυρὰ[8a] ἀνώχυρα[12] τοῖς ἐχθροῖς
καθίστη, τὰ μὲν παριών, τὰ δὲ ὑπερβαίνων, τὰ δὲ
κλέπτων.

and with remarkable caution.

7. Ὁπότε γε μὴν πορεύοιτο εἰδὼς ὅτι ἐξείη[43b] τοῖς
πολεμίοις μάχεσθαι, εἰ βούλοιντο, συντεταγμένον μὲν
οὕτως ἦγε τὸ στράτευμα ὡς ἂν ἐπικουρεῖν μάλιστα ἑαυτῷ
δύναιτο,[54b] ἡσύχως δὲ ὥσπερ ἂν παρθένος ἡ σωφρονεστάτη
προβαίνοι, νομίζων ἐν τῷ τοιούτῳ τό τε ἀτρεμὲς[5, 8a] καὶ
ἀνεκπληκτότατον καὶ ἀθορυβητότατον καὶ ἀναμαρτητό-
τατον καὶ δυσεπιβουλευτότατον εἶναι. 8. τοιγαροῦν
τοιαῦτα ποιῶν[58f] τοῖς μὲν πολεμίοις δεινὸς ἦν, τοῖς δὲ
φίλοις[16] θάρσος καὶ ῥώμην ἐνεποίει. ὥστε ἀκαταφρόνητος
μὲν ὑπὸ τῶν ἐχθρῶν διετέλεσεν,[49a] ἀζήμιος δ᾽ ὑπὸ τῶν
πολιτῶν, ἄμεμπτος δ᾽ ὑπὸ τῶν φίλων, πολυεραστότατος
δὲ καὶ πολυεπαινετώτατος ὑπὸ πάντων ἀνθρώπων.

CHAPTER VII.

His patriotism. He shrank from no toil, or hardship, or sacrifice, where the interests of his country were at stake.

1. "Ὡς γε μὴν φιλόπολις ἦν καθ' ἐν μὲν ἕκαστον μακρὸν ἂν εἴη[54b] γράφειν· οἴομαι γὰρ οὐδὲν εἶναι τῶν πεπραγμένων αὐτῷ[17c] ὅ,τι οὐκ εἰς τοῦτο συντείνει. ὡς δ' ἐν βραχεῖ εἰπεῖν,[29e] ἅπαντες ἐπιστάμεθα ὅτι Ἀγησίλαος, ὅπου ᾤετο[48] τὴν πατρίδα τι ὠφελήσειν, οὐ πόνων[24] ὑφίετο, οὐ κινδύνων ἀφίστατο, οὐ χρημάτων ἐφείδετο, οὐ σῶμα, οὐ γῆρας προὐφασίζετο, ἀλλὰ καὶ βασιλέως ἀγαθοῦ τοῦτο ἔργον ἐνόμιζε τὸ τοὺς ἀρχομένους ὡς πλεῖστα ἀγαθὰ[13] ποιεῖν.

He set to all an example of submission to law, and was as a father to his people.

2. Ἐν τοῖς μεγίστοις δὲ ὠφελήμασι τῆς πατρίδος καὶ τόδε ἐγὼ τίθημι αὐτοῦ, ὅτι δυνατώτατος ὢν[58d] ἐν τῇ πόλει φανερὸς ἦν μάλιστα τοῖς νόμοις λατρεύων.[59] τίς γὰρ ἂν ἠθέλησεν[63d] ἀπειθεῖν ὁρῶν[58c] τὸν βασιλέα πειθόμενον τίς δ' ἂν ἡγούμενος μειονεκτεῖν νεώτερόν τι ἐπεχείρησε ποιεῖν εἰδὼς τὸν βασιλέα νομίμως καὶ τὸ κρατεῖσθαι φέροντα; 3. ὃς καὶ πρὸς τοὺς διαφόρους ἐν τῇ πόλει ὥσπερ πατὴρ πρὸς παῖδας προσεφέρετο. ἐλοιδορεῖτο μὲν γὰρ ἐπὶ τοῖς ἁμαρτήμασιν, ἐτίμα δ' εἴ τι καλὸν πράττοιεν,[40b] παρίστατο δ' εἴ τις συμφορὰ συμβαίνοι, ἐχθρὸν[12] μὲν οὐδένα ἡγούμενος πολίτην, ἐπαινεῖν δὲ πάντας ἐθέλων, σώζεσθαι δὲ πάντας κέρδος νομίζων, ζημίαν δὲ τιθεὶς εἰ καὶ ὁ μικροῦ ἄξιος[25a] ἀπόλοιτο· εἰ δ' ἐν τοῖς νόμοις ἠρεμοῦντες διαμένοιεν, δῆλος ἦν εὐδαίμονα μὲν ἀεὶ ἔσεσθαι τὴν πατρίδα λογιζόμενος,[59] ἰσχυρὰν δὲ τότε ὅταν οἱ Ἕλληνες σωφρονῶσιν.[47]

29

But more than this, he was a true Greek. He would not allow Greeks to be enslaved by Greeks, and did all that he could to protect and deliver them from the Persian power.

4. Εἴ γε μὴν αὖ καλὸν Ἕλληνα ὄντα φιλέλληνα εἶναι, τίνα τις εἶδεν ἄλλον στρατηγὸν ἢ πόλιν οὐκ ἐθέλοντα⁴³ᶜ αἱρεῖν, ὅταν οἴηται³⁹ πορθήσειν, ἢ συμφορὰν νομίζοντα τὸ νικᾶν ἐν τῷ πρὸς Ἕλληνας πολέμῳ; 5. ἐκεῖνος τοίνυν, ἀγγελίας μὲν ἐλθούσης²⁷ αὐτῷ ὡς ἐν τῇ ἐν Κορίνθῳ μάχῃ ὀκτὼ μὲν Λακεδαιμονίων, ἐγγὺς δὲ μύριοι τῶν πολεμίων τεθναῖεν,⁴³ᵇ οὐκ ἐφησθεὶς⁵⁹ φανερὸς ἐγένετο, ἀλλ' εἶπεν ἄρα, Φεῦ, ὦ Ἑλλάς, ὁπότε οἱ νῦν τεθνηκότες ἱκανοὶ ἦσαν ζῶντες⁵⁸ᶜ νικᾶν μαχόμενοι⁵⁸ᶠ πάντας τοὺς βαρβάρους. 6. Κορινθίων γε μὴν τῶν φευγόντων λεγόντων ὅτι ἐνδιδοῖτο⁴³ᵇ αὐτοῖς ἡ πόλις, καὶ μηχανὰς ἐπιδεικνύντων αἷς πάντως ἤλπιζον ἑλεῖν τὰ τείχη, οὐκ ἤθελε προσβάλλειν, λέγων ὅτι οὐκ ἀνδραποδίζεσθαι δέοι Ἑλληνίδας πόλεις ἀλλὰ σωφρονίζειν. εἰ δὲ τοὺς ἁμαρτάνοντας, ἔφη, ἡμῶν αὐτῶν ἀφανιοῦμεν, ὁρᾶν χρὴ μὴ οὐδ' ἕξομεν⁴³ᵈ μεθ' ὅτου⁵⁰ᶜ τῶν βαρβάρων κρατήσομεν. 7. εἰ δ' αὖ καλὸν καὶ μισοπέρσην εἶναι, ὅτι καὶ ὁ πάλαι ἐξεστράτευσεν ὡς δουλωσόμενος⁵⁰ᵃ τὴν Ἑλλάδα καὶ ὁ νῦν συμμαχεῖ μὲν τούτοις¹⁶ μεθ' ὁποτέρων ἂν οἴηται³⁹ μείζω¹³ βλάψειν, δωρεῖται δ' ἐκείνοις οὓς ἂν νομίζῃ λαβόντας πλεῖστα κακὰ τοὺς Ἕλληνας ποιήσειν, εἰρήνην δὲ συμπράττει ἐξ ἧς ἂν ἡγῆται μάλιστα ἡμᾶς ἀλλήλοις¹⁶ πολεμήσειν· ὁρῶσι μὲν οὖν ἅπαντες ταῦτα· ἐπεμελήθη δέ τις ἄλλος πώποτε πλὴν Ἀγησίλαος ἢ ὅπως φῦλόν τι ἀποστήσεται⁵⁰ᵃ τοῦ Πέρσου ἢ ὅπως τὸ ἀποστὰν μὴ ἀπόληται ἢ τὸ παράπαν ὡς καὶ βασιλεὺς κακὰ ἔχων μὴ δυνήσεται τοῖς Ἕλλησι πράγματα παρέχειν; ὃς καὶ πολεμούσης τῆς πατρίδος πρὸς Ἕλληνας ὅμως τοῦ κοινοῦ ἀγαθοῦ²³ τῇ Ἑλλάδι οὐκ ἠμέλησεν, ἀλλ' ἐξέπλευσεν ὅ,τι δύναιτο κακὸν ποιήσων τὸν βάρβαρον.¹³

CHAPTER VIII.

His modesty and affable demeanour won him many friends.

1. Ἀλλὰ μὴν ἄξιόν γε αὐτοῦ καὶ τὸ εὔχαρι⁸ᵃ μὴ σιωπᾶσθαι· ᾧ γε ὑπαρχούσης μὲν τιμῆς,²⁷ παρούσης δὲ δυνάμεως, πρὸς δὲ τούτοις βασιλείας, καὶ ταύτης οὐκ ἐπιβουλευομένης ἀλλ᾽ ἀγαπωμένης, τὸ μὲν μεγάλαυχον οὐκ ἂν εἶδε⁵⁴ᵇ τις, τὸ δὲ φιλόστυργον καὶ θεραπευτικὸν τῶν φίλων²³ καὶ μὴ⁶² ζητῶν κατενόησεν ἄν. 2. διὰ δὲ τὸ εὔελπις⁹ καὶ εὔθυμος καὶ ἀεὶ ἱλαρὸς εἶναι πολλοὺς ἐποίει μὴ τοῦ⁶⁷ᵃ διαπράξασθαί τι μόνον ἕνεκα πλησιάζειν, ἀλλὰ καὶ τοῦ ἥδιον διημερεύειν. ἥκιστα δ᾽ ὢν οἷος μεγαληγορεῖν⁴⁹ᵃ ὅμως τῶν ἐπαινούντων²³ αὐτοὺς οὐ βαρέως ἤκουεν, ἡγούμενος βλάπτειν οὐδὲν αὐτούς, ὑπισχνεῖσθαι δὲ ἄνδρας ἀγαθοὺς ἔσεσθαι.

His high principle. He was inaccessible to bribes or to personal offers, and judged men not by what they could give, but by what they could do.

3. Ἀλλὰ μὴν καὶ τῇ μεγαλογνωμοσύνῃ γε ὡς εὐκαίρως ἐχρῆτο οὐ παραλειπτέον.³¹ᵃ ἐκεῖνος γὰρ ὅτ᾽ ἦλθεν αὐτῷ ἐπιστολὴ παρὰ βασιλέως, ἣν ὁ μετὰ Καλλέα τοῦ Λακεδαιμονίου Πέρσης⁸ ἤνεγκε, περὶ ξενίας τε καὶ φιλίας αὐτοῦ, ταύτην μὲν οὐκ ἐδέξατο, τῷ δὲ φέροντι εἶπεν ἀπαγγεῖλαι⁴⁴ βασιλεῖ ὡς ἰδίᾳ μὲν πρὸς αὐτὸν οὐδὲν δέοι ἐπιστολὰς πέμπειν, ἢν δὲ φίλος τῇ Λακεδαίμονι καὶ τῇ Ἑλλάδι εὔνους ὢν φαίνηται, ὅτι καὶ αὐτὸς φίλος ἀνὰ κράτος αὐτῷ ἔσοιτο·⁴³ᵇ ἢν μέντοι, ἔφη, ἐπιβουλεύων ἁλίσκηται, μηδ᾽ ἂν πάνυ πολλὰς ἐπιστολὰς δέχωμαι, φίλον ἕξειν⁵⁵,⁵³ᵇ με οἰέσθω. 4. ἐγὼ οὖν καὶ τοῦτο ἐπαινῶ Ἀγησιλάου τὸ πρὸς τὸ ἀρέσκειν τοῖς Ἕλλησιν

ὑπεριδεῖν τὴν βασιλέως ξενίαν. ἄγαμαι δὲ κἀκεῖνο ὅτι
οὐχ ὁπότερος πλείω τε χρήματα ἔχοι καὶ πλειόνων
ἄρχοι, τούτῳ[31a] ἡγήσατο μεῖζον φρονητέον εἶναι, ἀλλ'
ὁπότερος αὐτός τε ἀμείνων εἴη καὶ ἀμεινόνων ἡγοῖτο.
5. ἐπαινῶ δὲ κἀκεῖνο τῆς προνοίας[21a] αὐτοῦ ὅτι νομίζων
ἀγαθὸν τῇ Ἑλλάδι ἀφίστασθαι[29a] τοῦ βασιλέως ὡς
πλείστους σατράπας, οὐκ ἐκρατήθη οὔθ' ὑπὸ δώρων οὔθ'
ὑπὸ τῆς βασιλέως ῥώμης ἐθελῆσαι ξενωθῆναι αὐτῷ,
ἀλλ' ἐφυλάξατο μὴ[65] ἄπιστος γενέσθαι τοῖς ἀφίστασθαι
βουλομένοις.

*His carelessness of personal aggrandisement and absence of display
—shown by his modest style of living.*

6. Ἐκεῖνό γε μὴν αὐτοῦ τίς οὐκ ἂν ἀγασθείη;[54b] ὁ μὲν
γὰρ Πέρσης, νομίζων, ἢν χρήματα πλεῖστα ἔχῃ, πάνθ'
ὑφ' ἑαυτῷ ποιήσεσθαι,[53b,55] διὰ τοῦτο πᾶν μὲν τὸ ἐν
ἀνθρώποις χρυσίον, πᾶν δὲ τὸ ἀργύριον, πάντα δὲ τὰ
πολυτελέστατα ἐπειρᾶτο πρὸς ἑαυτὸν ἀθροίζειν. ὁ δὲ
οὕτως ἀντεσκευάσατο τὸν οἶκον ὥστε τούτων μηδενὸς[26a]
προσδεῖσθαι. 7. εἰ δέ τις ταῦτα ἀπιστεῖ, ἰδέτω μὲν οἵα
οἰκία ἤρκει αὐτῷ, θεασάσθω δὲ τὰς θύρας αὐτοῦ· εἰκάσειε
γὰρ ἄν τις ἔτι ταύτας ἐκείνας εἶναι ἅσπερ Ἀριστόδημος ὁ
Ἡρακλέους ὅτε κατῆλθε[52] λαβὼν ἐπεστήσατο· πειράσθω
δὲ θεάσασθαι τὴν ἔνδον κατασκευήν, ἐννοησάτω δὲ ὡς
ἐθοίναζεν ἐν ταῖς θυσίαις, ἀκουσάτω δὲ ὡς ἐπὶ πολιτικοῦ
κανάθρου κατῄει εἰς Ἀμύκλας ἡ θυγάτηρ αὐτοῦ. 8.
τοιγαροῦν οὕτως ἐφαρμόσας τὰς δαπάνας ταῖς προσόδοις[18]
οὐδὲν ἠναγκάζετο χρημάτων ἕνεκα ἄδικον πράττειν.
καίτοι καλὸν μὲν δοκεῖ εἶναι τείχη ἀνάλωτα κτᾶσθαι
ὑπὸ πολεμίων· πολὺ μέντοι ἔγωγε κάλλιον κρίνω τὸ
τὴν αὐτοῦ ψυχὴν ἀνάλωτον κατασκευάσαι καὶ ὑπὸ χρημάτων καὶ ὑπὸ ἡδονῶν καὶ ὑπὸ φόβου.

32

CHAPTER IX.

*This last feature becomes more marked, if his Spartan simplicity
is contrasted with the luxury of the Persian Court.*

1. Ἀλλὰ μὴν ἐρῶ γε ὡς καὶ τὸν τρόπον ὑπεστήσατο
τῇ τοῦ Πέρσου ἀλαζονείᾳ.[16] πρῶτον μὲν γὰρ ὁ μὲν τῷ
σπανίως ὁρᾶσθαι ἐσεμνύνετο, Ἀγησίλαος δὲ τῷ ἀεὶ
ἐμφανὴς[9] εἶναι ἠγάλλετο, νομίζων αἰσχρουργίᾳ μὲν τὸ
ἀφανίζεσθαι πρέπειν, τῷ δὲ εἰς κάλλος βίῳ[16] τὸ φῶς μᾶλλον
κόσμον παρέχειν. 2. ἔπειτα δὲ ὁ μὲν τῷ δυσπρόσοδος
εἶναι[19a] ἐσεμνύνετο, ὁ δὲ τῷ πᾶσιν εὐπρόσοδος εἶναι ἔχαιρε·
καὶ ὁ μὲν ἡβρύνετο τῷ βραδέως διαπράττειν,[30] ὁ δὲ τότε
μάλιστα ἔχαιρεν ὁπότε τάχιστα τυχόντας ὧν δέοιντο
ἀποπέμποι. 3. ἀλλὰ μὴν καὶ τὴν εὐπάθειαν ὅσῳ ῥάονα
καὶ εὐπορωτέραν Ἀγησίλαος ἐπετήδευσεν ἄξιον κατα-
νοῆσαι. τῷ μὲν γὰρ Πέρσῃ[17] πᾶσαν γῆν περιέρχονται
μαστεύοντες τί ἂν ἡδέως πίοι,[54b] μυρίοι δὲ τεχνῶνται τί
ἂν ἡδέως φάγοι· ὅπως γε μὴν καταδάρθοι[50] οὐδ᾽ ἂν εἴποι
τις ὅσα πραγματεύονται. Ἀγησίλαος δὲ διὰ τὸ φιλό-
πονος εἶναι πᾶν μὲν τὸ παρὸν ἡδέως ἔπινε, πᾶν δὲ τὸ
συντυχὸν ἡδέως ἤσθιεν· εἰς δὲ τὸ ἀσμένως κοιμηθῆναι
πᾶς τόπος ἱκανὸς ἦν αὐτῷ. 4. καὶ ταῦτα οὐ μόνον
πράττων[59] ἔχαιρεν, ἀλλὰ καὶ ἐνθυμούμενος ἠγάλλετο ὅτι
αὐτὸς μὲν ἐν μέσαις ταῖς εὐφροσύναις ἀναστρέφοιτο τὸν
δὲ βάρβαρον ἑώρα, εἰ μέλλοι ἀλύπως βιώσεσθαι, συνελ-
κυστέον αὐτῷ[31] ἀπὸ περάτων τῆς γῆς τὰ τέρψοντα. 5.
εὔφραινε δὲ αὐτὸν καὶ τάδε ὅτι αὐτὸς μὲν ᾔδει τῇ τῶν θεῶν
κατασκευῇ δυνάμενος[43b] ἀλύπως χρῆσθαι, τὸν δὲ ἑώρα
φεύγοντα μὲν θάλπη, φεύγοντα δὲ ψύχη, δι᾽ ἀσθένειαν
ψυχῆς, οὐκ ἀνδρῶν ἀγαθῶν ἀλλὰ θηρίων τῶν ἀσθενεσ-
τάτων βίον μιμούμενον.

33

The distinctions in games and the like, that most of the Greeks coveted, he set no store upon, preferring to be honoured for his deeds and his life.

6. Ἐκεῖνό γε μὴν πῶς οὐ καλὸν καὶ μεγαλόγνωμον, τὸ αὐτὸν μὲν ἀνδρὸς ἔργοις καὶ κτήμασι[19a] κοσμεῖν τὸν ἑαυτοῦ οἶκον, κύνας τε πολλοὺς θηρευτὰς καὶ ἵππους πολεμιστηρίους τρέφοντα, Κυνίσκαν δὲ ἀδελφὴν οὖσαν πεῖσαί ἁρματοτροφεῖν καὶ ἐπιδεῖξαι νικώσης αὐτῆς[27] ὅτι τὸ θρέμμα τοῦτο οὐκ ἀνδραγαθίας ἀλλὰ πλούτου ἐπίδειγμά ἐστι. 7. τόδε γε μὴν πῶς οὐ σαφῶς πρὸς τὸ γενναῖον ἔγνω ὅτι ἅρματι μὲν νικήσας τοὺς ἰδιώτας οὐδὲν ὀνομαστότερος ἂν γένοιτο, εἰ δὲ φίλην μὲν πάντων μάλιστα τὴν πόλιν ἔχοι, πλείστους δὲ φίλους καὶ ἀρίστους ἀνὰ πᾶσαν τὴν γῆν κεκτῆτο, νικῴη δὲ τὴν μὲν πατρίδα καὶ τοὺς ἑταίρους εὐεργετῶν, τοὺς δὲ ἀντιπάλους τιμωρούμενος, ὅτι ὄντως ἂν εἴη νικηφόρος τῶν καλλίστων καὶ μεγαλοπρεπεστάτων ἀγωνισμάτων καὶ ὀνομαστότατος καὶ ζῶν καὶ τελευτήσας[58b] γένοιτ᾽ ἄν;

CHAPTER X.

Value of such an example, as inciting others to the same life of justice, and temperance and self-control.

1. Ἐγὼ μὲν οὖν τὰ τοιαῦτα[13] ἐπαινῶ Ἀγησίλαον. ταῦτα γὰρ οὐχ ὥσπερ εἰ θησαυρῷ[16] τις ἐντύχοι, πλουσιώτερος μὲν ἂν εἴη, οἰκονομικώτερος δ᾽ οὐδὲν ἄν, καὶ εἰ νόσου δὲ πολεμίοις ἐμπεσούσης[58a] κρατήσειεν, εὐτυχέστερος μὲν ἂν εἴη, στρατηγικώτερος δὲ οὐδὲν ἄν· ὁ δὲ καρτερίᾳ μὲν πρωτεύων ἔνθα πονεῖν καιρός, ἀλκῇ δὲ ὅπου ἀνδρείας ἀγών, γνώμῃ δὲ ὅπου βουλῆς ἔργον, οὗτος

ἔμοιγε δοκεῖ δικαίως ἀνὴρ ἀγαθὸς παντελῶς ἂν νομίζε-
σθαι.[55] 2. εἰ δὲ καλὸν εὕρημα ἀνθρώποις στάθμη καὶ
κανὼν πρὸς τὸ ἀγαθὰ ἐργάζεσθαι, καλὸν ἄν μοι δοκεῖ ἡ
Ἀγησιλάου ἀρετὴ παράδειγμα γενέσθαι τοῖς ἀνδραγαθίαν
ἀσκεῖν βουλομένοις. τίς γὰρ ἂν ἢ θεοσεβῆ μιμούμενος[58f]
ἀνόσιος γένοιτο ἢ δίκαιον ἄδικος ἢ σώφρονα ὑβριστὴς ἢ
ἐγκρατῆ ἀκρατής ; | καὶ γὰρ δὴ οὐχ οὕτως ἐπὶ τῷ ἄλλων
βασιλεύειν ὡς ἐπὶ τῷ ἑαυτοῦ[25] ἄρχειν ἐμεγαλύνετο, οὐδ᾽
ἐπὶ τῷ πρὸς τοὺς πολεμίους ἀλλ᾽ ἐπὶ τῷ πρὸς πᾶσαν
ἀρετὴν ἡγεῖσθαι τοῖς πολίταις.[17] 3. ἀλλὰ γὰρ μὴ ὅτι
τετελευτηκὼς[58b] ἐπαινεῖται τούτου ἕνεκα θρῆνόν τις
τοῦτον τὸν λόγον νομισάτω, ἀλλὰ πολὺ μᾶλλον ἐγκώμιον.
πρῶτον μὲν γὰρ ἅπερ ζῶν ἤκουε, ταῦτα καὶ νῦν λέγεται
περὶ αὐτοῦ. ἔπειτα δὲ τί καὶ πλέον θρήνου[24] ἄπεστιν
ἢ βίος τε εὐκλεὴς καὶ θάνατος ὡραῖος ; ἐγκωμίων[25a] δὲ τί
ἀξιώτερον ἢ νῖκαί τε αἱ κάλλισται καὶ ἔργα τὰ πλείστου
ἄξια ; 4. δικαίως δ᾽ ἂν ἐκεῖνός γε μακαρίζοιτο[54b] ὃς εὐθὺς
μὲν ἐκ παιδὸς ἐρασθεὶς τοῦ εὐκλεὴς γενέσθαι ἔτυχε τούτου
μάλιστα τῶν καθ᾽ ἑαυτόν·[21,8a] φιλοτιμότατος δὲ πεφυκὼς
ἀήττητος διετέλεσεν, ἐπεὶ[52] βασιλεὺς ἐγένετο. ἀφικόμενος
δὲ ἐπὶ τὸ μήκιστον ἀνθρωπίνου αἰῶνος ἀναμάρτητος
ἐτελεύτησε καὶ περὶ τούτους ὧν[25] ἡγεῖτο καὶ πρὸς ἐκείνους
οἷς ἐπολέμει.

CHAPTER XI.

*General recapitulation.   Agesilaus' regard for holy
places and things.*

1. Βούλομαι δὲ καὶ ἐν κεφαλαίοις ἐπανελθεῖν τὴν
ἀρετὴν αὐτοῦ, ὡς ἂν ὁ ἔπαινος εὐμνημονεστέρως ἔχῃ.[50]
Ἀγησίλαος ἱερὰ μὲν καὶ τὰ ἐν τοῖς πολεμίοις ἐσέβετο,
ἡγούμενος τοὺς θεοὺς οὐχ ἧττον ἐν τῇ πολεμίᾳ χρῆναι[43a]

ἢ ἐν τῇ φιλίᾳ συμμάχους ποιεῖσθαι. ἱκέτας δὲ θεῶν[22]
οὐδὲ ἐχθροὺς ἐβιάζετο, νομίζων ἄλογον εἶναι τοὺς μὲν ἐξ
ἱερῶν κλέπτοντας ἱεροσύλους καλεῖν, τοὺς δὲ βωμῶν[24]
ἱκέτας ἀποσπῶντας εὐσεβεῖς ἡγεῖσθαι. 2. ἐκεῖνός γε
μὴν ὑμνῶν[59] οὔποτ᾽ ἔληγεν ὡς τοὺς θεοὺς οἴοιτο οὐδὲν
ἧττον ὁσίοις ἔργοις[16] ἢ ἁγνοῖς ἱεροῖς ἥδεσθαι. ἀλλὰ μὴν
καὶ ὁπότε εὐτυχοίη,[40b] οὐκ ἀνθρώπων ὑπερεφρόνει, ἀλλὰ
θεοῖς χάριν ᾔδει. καὶ θαρρῶν πλείονα ἔθυεν ἢ ὀκνῶν
ηὔχετο. εἴθιστο δὲ φοβούμενος[58b] μὲν ἱλαρὸς φαίνεσθαι,
εὐτυχῶν δὲ πρᾷος εἶναι.

*His love for all that is noble and upright, and detestation of
ingratitude and meanness.*

3. τῶν γε μὴν φίλων[21a] οὐ τοὺς δυνατωτάτους ἀλλὰ
τοὺς προθυμοτάτους μάλιστα ἠσπάζετο. ἐμίσει δὲ οὐκ εἴ
τις κακῶς πάσχων ἠμύνετο, ἀλλ᾽ εἴ τις εὐεργετούμενος
ἀχάριστος φαίνοιτο.[36] ἔχαιρε δὲ τοὺς μὲν αἰσχροκερδεῖς
πένητας ὁρῶν,[59] τοὺς δὲ δικαίους πλουσίους ποιῶν, βουλόμενος τὴν δικαιοσύνην τῆς ἀδικίας[25] κερδαλεωτέραν καθιστάναι. 4. ἤσκει δὲ ἐξομιλεῖν μὲν παντοδαποῖς, χρῆσθαι
δὲ τοῖς ἀγαθοῖς. ὁπότε δὲ ψεγόντων ἢ ἐπαινούντων[23]
τινὰς ἀκούοι, οὐχ ἧττον ᾤετο καταμανθάνειν τοὺς τῶν
λεγόντων τρόπους ἢ περὶ ὧν λέγοιεν. καὶ τοὺς μὲν ὑπὸ
φίλων ἐξαπατωμένους[8a] οὐκ ἔψεγε, τοὺς δὲ ὑπὸ πολεμίων
πάμπαν κατεμέμφετο, καὶ τὸ μὲν ἀπιστοῦντας ἐξαπατᾶν
σοφὸν ἔκρινε, τὸ δὲ πιστεύοντας ἀνόσιον.

*His love of open criticism, and hatred of slander, and stern view
of the responsibilities of men in power.*

5. ἐπαινούμενος δὲ ἔχαιρεν ὑπὸ τῶν καὶ ψέγειν ἐθελόν-
των τὰ μὴ[62b] ἀρεστά, καὶ τῶν παρρησιαζομένων οὐδένα
ἤχθραινε, τοὺς δὲ κρυψίνους ὥσπερ ἐνέδρας ἐφυλάττετο.

τούς γε μὴν διαβόλους μᾶλλον ἢ τοὺς κλέπτας ἐμίσει, μείζω ζημίαν ἡγούμενος φίλων ἢ χρημάτων²⁴ στερίσκεσθαι. 6. καὶ τὰς μὲν τῶν ἰδιωτῶν ἁμαρτίας πράως ἔφερε, τὰς δὲ τῶν ἀρχόντων μεγάλας ἦγε κρίνων τοὺς μὲν ὀλίγα, τοὺς δὲ πολλὰ κακῶς διατιθέναι. τῇ δὲ βασιλείᾳ προσήκειν ἐνόμιζεν οὐ ῥᾳδιουργίαν ἀλλὰ καλοκἀγαθίαν.

His modesty, liberality, and religiousness.

7. καὶ τοῦ μὲν σώματος εἰκόνα στήσασθαι ἀπέσχετο, πολλῶν αὐτῷ τοῦτο δωρεῖσθαι θελόντων, τῆς δὲ ψυχῆς οὐδέποτε ἐπαύετο μνημεῖα διαπονούμενος,⁵⁹ ἡγούμενος τὸ μὲν ἀνδριαντοποιῶν, τὸ δὲ αὐτοῦ ἔργον εἶναι, καὶ τὸ μὲν πλουσίων, τὸ δὲ τῶν ἀγαθῶν. 8. χρήμασί γε μὴν οὐ μόνον δικαίως ἀλλὰ καὶ ἐλευθερίως ἐχρῆτο, τῷ μὲν δικαίῳ ἀρκεῖν ἡγούμενος τὸ ἐᾶν³⁰ τὰ ἀλλότρια, τῷ δὲ ἐλευθερίῳ καὶ τῶν ἑαυτοῦ²¹ προσωφελητέον³¹ εἶναι. ἀεὶ δὲ δεισιδαίμων ἦν, νομίζων τοὺς μὲν καλῶς ζῶντας οὔπω εὐδαίμονας, τοὺς δὲ εὐκλεῶς τετελευτηκότας ἤδη μακαρίους. 9. μείζω δὲ συμφορὰν ἔκρινε τὸ γιγνώσκοντα ἢ ἀγνοοῦντα⁹ ἀμελεῖν τῶν ἀγαθῶν· δόξης δὲ οὐδεμιᾶς ἤρα ἧς οὐκ ἐξεπόνει τὰ ἴδια. μετ᾽ ὀλίγων δέ μοι ἐδόκει ἀνθρώπων οὐ καρτερίαν τὴν ἀρετὴν ἀλλ᾽ εὐπάθειαν νομίζειν· ἐπαινούμενος⁵⁹ γοῦν ἔχαιρε μᾶλλον ἢ χρήματα κτώμενος. ἀλλὰ μὴν ἀνδρείαν γε τὸ πλέον μετ᾽ εὐβουλίας ἢ μετὰ κινδύνων ἐπεδείκνυτο, καὶ σοφίαν ἔργῳ μᾶλλον ἢ λόγοις¹⁹ᵃ ἤσκει.

He was a kindly friend, and a formidable foe, though ever lenient in victory; a helper to the needy, affectionate to his kinsmen, grateful for service.

10. Πρᾳότατός γε μὴν φίλοις ὢν ἐχθροῖς¹⁷ φοβερώτατος ἦν· καὶ πόνοις μάλιστα ἀντέχων ἑταίροις ἥδιστα ὑπεῖκε,

καλῶν ἔργων[23] μᾶλλον ἢ τῶν καλῶν σωμάτων ἐπιθυμῶν.
ἔν γε μὴν ταῖς εὐπραξίαις σωφρονεῖν ἐπιστάμενος ἐν τοῖς
δεινοῖς εὐθαρσὴς ἐδύνατο εἶναι. 11. καὶ τὸ εὔχαρι οὐ
σκώμμασιν ἀλλὰ τρόπῳ ἐπετήδευε, καὶ τῷ μεγαλόφρονι
οὐ σὺν ὕβρει ἀλλὰ σὺν γνώμῃ ἐχρῆτο· τῶν γοῦν ὑπεραύ-
χων[23] καταφρονῶν τῶν μετρίων ταπεινότερος ἦν. καὶ γὰρ
ἐκαλλωπίζετο τῇ μὲν ἀμφὶ τὸ σῶμα φαυλότητι,[8] τῷ δ'
ἀμφὶ τὸ στράτευμα κόσμῳ· τῷ δ' αὐτὸς[9] μὲν ὡς ἐλαχίστων
δεῖσθαι, τοὺς δὲ φίλους ὡς πλεῖστα ὠφελεῖν. 12. πρὸς
δὲ τούτοις βαρύτατος μὲν ἀνταγωνιστὴς ἦν, κουφότατος
δὲ κρατήσας· ἐχθροῖς μὲν δυσεξαπάτητος, φίλοις δὲ
εὐπαραπειστότατος. ἀεὶ δὲ τιθεὶς τὰ τῶν φίλων ἀσφαλῶς
ἀεὶ ἀμαυροῦν τὰ τῶν πολεμίων ἔργον εἶχεν. 13. ἐκεῖνον
οἱ μὲν συγγενεῖς φιλοκηδεμόνα ἐκάλουν, οἱ δὲ χρώμενοι
ἀπροφάσιστον, οἱ δ' ὑπουργήσαντές τι μνήμονα, οἱ δ'
ἀδικούμενοι ἐπίκουρον, οἵ γε μὴν συγκινδυνεύοντες μετὰ
θεοὺς σωτῆρα.

*He was a noble specimen of a vigorous old age, for even when past
military service, his activity in other ways made him respected
and feared.*

14. Δοκεῖ δ' ἔμοιγε καὶ τόδε μόνος ἀνθρώπων ἐπιδεῖξαι
ὅτι ἡ μὲν τοῦ σώματος ἰσχὺς γηράσκει, ἡ δὲ τῆς ψυχῆς
ῥώμη τῶν ἀγαθῶν ἀνδρῶν ἀγήρατός ἐστιν. ἐκεῖνος γοῦν
οὐκ ἀπεῖπε μεγάλην καὶ καλὴν ἐφιέμενος[59] δόξαν, εἰ καὶ
μὴ τὸ σῶμα φέρειν ἠδύνατο τὴν τῆς ψυχῆς αὐτοῦ ῥώμην.
15. τοιγαροῦν ποίας οὐ νεότητος[25] κρεῖττον τὸ ἐκείνου
γῆρας ἐφάνη; τίς μὲν γὰρ τοῖς ἐχθροῖς ἀκμάζων οὕτω
φοβερὸς ἦν ὡς Ἀγησίλαος τὸ μήκιστον τοῦ αἰῶνος ἔχων;
τίνος δ' ἐκποδὼν γενομένου[27] μᾶλλον ἤσθησαν οἱ πολέμιοι
ἢ Ἀγησιλάου καίπερ γηραιοῦ τελευτήσαντος; τίς δὲ
ξυμμάχοις θάρσος παρέσχεν ὅσον Ἀγησίλαος, καίπερ ἤδη

πρὸς τῷ στόματι τοῦ βίου ὤν ;[58d] τίνα δὲ νέον οἱ φίλοι
πλέον ἐπόθησαν ἢ ᾿Αγησίλαον γηραιὸν ἀποθανόντα ;
16. οὕτω δὲ τελέως ὁ ἀνὴρ τῇ πατρίδι ὠφέλιμος ὢν[59]
διεγένετο ὡς καὶ τετελευτηκὼς ἤδη ἔτι μεγαλείως ὠφελῶν
τὴν πόλιν εἰς τὴν ἀΐδιον οἴκησιν κατηγάγετο,[19, Obs.] μνημεῖα
μὲν τῆς ἑαυτοῦ ἀρετῆς ἀνὰ πᾶσαν τὴν γῆν κτησάμενος,
τῆς δὲ βασιλικῆς ταφῆς[23] ἐν τῇ πατρίδι τυχών.

Observation.—The rules that follow are written, as far as differences of idiom will allow, on the lines of the First Memorial Syntax in the Public School Latin Primer, which it is supposed that the pupil will have learnt. Some few rules, such as those on the Composite Subject, have consequently been omitted.

On Agreement.

1. A Finite Verb agrees with its Subject in Number and Person.

Exceptions.—(*a*) A Plural Subject of the neuter gender is followed by a verb in the singular; ἄβατά ἐστι τὰ ὄρη, 'the mountains are impassable.'

(*b*) A Dual Subject of the masculine or feminine gender may be followed by a verb in the plural, ὡς εἰδέτην ἀλλήλους ἡ γυνὴ καὶ ὁ 'Αβραδάτης, ἠσπάσαντο ἀλλήλους.—XEN.

(*c*) A Singular Subject, implying multitude, may be followed by a plural verb, when the act is done by the individuals and not by the body as a whole, τὸ πλῆθος οἴονται (THUC. i. 20), 'the multitude think.' The following is a good example of the two constructions :—τὸ στράτευμα ἐπορίζετο σῖτον, κόπτοντες τοὺς βοῦς (XEN. *Anab.* ii. 1. 6), where the army provided itself with meat, but individual soldiers were the butchers.

(*d*) The verb is sometimes attracted to the number of the complement.

2. An Adjective or Participle agrees with that to which it is in attribution in number, gender, and case.

Exc.—(*a*) A neuter adjective may be added as predicate to a masculine or feminine noun, when it denotes an essential quality, *e.g.* ἀσθενέστερον γυνὴ ἀνδρός, 'a woman is a weaker (creature) than a man.'

(*b*) The adjective belonging to the subject is sometimes attracted to the gender of the complement, as ἦσαν δὲ ταῦτα δύο τείχη (XEN. *Anab.* i. 4. 4), where ταῦτα = αἱ πύλαι.

3. A Substantive agrees in case with that to which it is in apposition.

D

4. A Relative agrees with its antecedent in number, gender, and person, but in case follows its own clause.

    (*a*) When a Relative would naturally be in the *Accusative* case, and the Antecedent in the Genitive or Dative, the Relative frequently takes the case of the Antecedent. This is called the Relative Attraction. It is only used when the Relative Sentence is purely adjectival, *i.e.* when it simply defines its Antecedent. If the Antecedent is a demonstrative pronoun or adjective, it is in this case often omitted; σὺν οἶς (= σὺν ἐκείνοις οὕς) μάλιστα φιλεῖς.—XEN. *Anab.* i. 9. 25.

    (*b*) A Neuter Relative frequently refers to a sentence as its Antecedent.

    (*c*) The Antecedent is often drawn into the Relative Clause, and takes the case of the Relative; κατασκευάζοντα ἧς ἄρχοι χώρας, 'developing the resources of the province which he governed' (= τὴν χώραν ἧς ἄρχοι).—XEN. *Anab.* i. 9. 19.

The Use of the Article.

5. The Article, ὁ, ἡ, τό, marks the Substantive to which it is prefixed as a definite or known object.

    (*a*) Hence, if an adjective be attached as an attributive *epithet* to define a noun with the Article, it must immediately follow the article, or have the article repeated with it; otherwise it becomes an attributive *complement*; ὁ μέγας βασιλεύς or ὁ βασιλεύς ὁ μέγας, 'the great king;' μέγας ὁ βασιλεύς, '.the king is great.' So the Article distinguishes the Subject from the Predicate; καλός ἐστιν ὁ παῖς, 'the lad is handsome,' καλός ἐστι παῖς, 'he is a handsome lad.'

    (*b*) By this use of the Article a simple sentence may be made to contain two predications, one concerning the subject, the other concerning the object, or some other noun in an oblique case. Such a sentence may often best be translated by the use of a relative clause, *e.g.* τοσοῦτον εἶχε τὸ στράτευμα ὁ Κῦρος, 'so great was the army which Cyrus had.' A predicate which thus refers to an oblique case is called a *tertiary predicate.*

    (*c*) The Adjectives μέσος, ἄκρος, ἥμισυς, and others, are thus used predicatively, where we should use a substantive,—*e.g.* ἄκρα ἡ χείρ, 'the tip of the hand.' Compare the Latin use of *summus, medius,* etc., L. P. p. 139.

6. The Article distinguishes *individuals*, as different from others of the same class, or as having been before mentioned, or by their qualities or belongings; hence it may frequently be translated by the Possessive Pronoun, as τὰς χεῖρας ἀνέτεινε, 'he held up his hands.'

    (*a*) Hence it is always added to οὗτος, ὅδε, and ἐκεῖνος.

7. The Article *generalises*, or, in other words, puts the individual forward as the representative of its class, ὁ σοφιστής, ὁ διδάσκων, 'the teacher.' It may often be translated by the English indefinite article, *e.g.* δεῖ τὸν στρατιώτην πείθεσθαι τῷ ἄρχοντι, 'a soldier must obey his officer.'

8. All words which come between the Article and the noun to which it belongs are epithets, and describe the noun.

(*a.*) Hence the Article is put with adjectives, participles, adverbs, and oblique cases of nouns with or without prepositions, to denote persons and things whose qualities or relations they express, the noun to be supplied being easily understood : *e.g.* οἱ σοφοί, 'the 'wise (class of men),' τὸ αἰσχρόν, 'meanness,' οἱ πολιτευόμενοι, 'statesmen,' οἱ νῦν, 'the present generation,' οἱ ἀμφὶ τὸν Κῦρον, 'Cyrus' company.'

A Participle with the Article is generally best translated by a Relative Clause, as ὁ λύων, 'the man who is loosing,' τὸν βασιλεύοντα Ἀρταξέρξην, 'Artaxerxes, who was king.'

The Cases.

9. The Subject and the Complement of a Finite Verb are put in the Nominative case ; the Subject and the Complement to an Infinitive are generally put in the Accusative (cf. § 18).

But where the infinitive and the principal verb have the same subject, the Nominative is retained throughout ; as οὐκ ἔφη αὐτὸς ἀλλὰ Νικίαν στρατηγεῖν, 'he said that not he, but Nicias was general.'

The Accusative.

10. The Accusative denotes the limit towards which, or the space over which, a thing moves, or an action is directed, or describes the action that is done. It is the case of the nearer object.

11. Transitive Verbs govern an Accusative of the object.

12. Factitive Verbs, as of making, calling, thinking, have a second Accusative of the Complement. See § 5 (*b*). Δαρεῖος Κῦρον σατράπην ἐποίησε, 'Darius made Cyrus satrap.'—XEN. *Anab.* i. 1. 2.

13. In Greek any Verb, transitive or intransitive, with the exception of Substantive verbs, can take an Accusative of its own *contents*, which is sometimes called an *Accusative of kindred meaning*, or an *Accusative of the action of the verb*. In the case of transitive verbs, this Accusative is retained in the passive, *e.g.* ταῦτά σε ἠδίκηκα, 'I have done you this wrong;' passive, ταῦτα σὺ ἠδίκησαι. With intransitive verbs, it sometimes becomes the subject to a passive form, πολλὰ σὺ ἡμάρτηκας, 'you have committed many blunders;' passive, πολλὰ ἡμάρτηταί σοι, or ὑπὸ σοῦ.

43

(*a*) Hence many verbs of asking, teaching, concealing, clothing, depriving, etc., take two Accusatives, one of the person, the other of the thing ; ἀφαιρεῖσθαι τοὺς οἰκοῦντας Ἕλληνας τὴν γῆν, 'to take away the land from the Greeks who were inhabiting it.' —XEN. *Anab.* i. 3. 4.

14. The Accusative of Extent is used after verbs, participles, and adjectives, to express—

(*a*) Measure of space and time, answering to the questions, How far ? How long ? διεῖχον ἀλλήλων ὡς τριάκοντα στάδια.—XEN. *Anab.* i. 2. 4. ἔμεινεν ἡμέρας πέντε, i. 2. 6.

(*b*) The object in respect of which what is stated about the subject is true, *i.e.* how far it extends (Accusative of Respect), ἀλγῶ τὴν κεφαλήν, 'I have an aching in the head, a headache.'

The Dative.

15. The fundamental notion of the Dative case is that of nearness and contact. It is the case of the Recipient, and also expresses some relations which are expressed by the Latin Ablative.

16. The Dative of the Recipient follows all words which imply actual nearness, or the bringing of a thing near to body or mind. Such are words which express likeness or unlikeness, agreement and disagreement, friendliness and hostility, advantage and disadvantage, pleasing and displeasing ; and verbs of giving, showing, telling, and obeying, and their contraries.

17. The Dative may be added anywhere to mark the person concerned in the doing of an action, or the existence of a quality, or for whose interest the action takes place or the quality exists, *e.g.* Σόλων τοῖς Ἀθηναίοις νόμους ἔθηκε, 'Solon made laws for the Athenians;' τέθνηκα ὑμῖν, 'I am dead as far as your interest in me goes.' To this head belong—

(*a*) The Dative of the Personal Pronoun, which refers to the whole sentence rather than to any particular word in it, and is called the Ethic Dative ; τί σοι μαθήσομαι, 'what would you have me learn ?'

(*b*) The Dative with ἔστι, γίγνεται, which implies possession or gain.

(*c*) The Dative, used for the case of the Agent after Verbal Adjectives in -τεος and -τος, and after Passive verbs, especially in the Perfect and Pluperfect ; the doer of the action being most concerned in the action necessary or possible to be done, and in the fruit of it when completed. ὠφελητέα σοι ἡ πόλις ἐστίν, 'you must help your country,' XEN. ; τί πέπρακται τοῖς ἄλλοις ; 'what has been done, as far as the others are concerned ?'

18. A Dative is sometimes used by Attraction as Complement to an Infinitive which is referred to a word in the sentence, that is in the Dative, as its subject ; as εὐδαίμοσιν ὑμῖν ἔξεστι γίγνεσθαι, 'it is open to you to become prosperous.'

19. The Dative takes the place of the Latin Ablative in expressing—

(*a*) The instrument, cause, or manner of an action : τοῖς μήκεσι τῶν ὁδῶν ἀσθενής, 'weak because of the great distances.'

(*b*) The measure of excess or defect : πολλῷ μεῖζον, 'much greater ;'

(*c*) The place where (rarely in prose), or the time when, an action occurs : Μαραθῶνι, 'at Marathon' (really Locative), τετάρτῳ ἔτει, 'in the fourth year.

The Genitive.

20. The idea that underlies the Genitive case is that of detachment or separation.   It is the classifying case, or the case of predication, and is in many instances equivalent to an adjective, or to the first member of an English compound noun, as λόγων ἀγών, 'a word-contest ;' κρᾶνος χαλκοῦ, 'a brazen helmet.'

21. The Subjective Genitive denotes the Author or Possessor, or that to which an action or quality belongs, or is natural.

(*a*) A Genitive of Partition, or of the thing measured or distributed, is added to numerals and superlatives, and to words of quantity, and also to words which imply *sharing.* πάντων ἄριστος, 'bravest of all.' μετεδίδοσαν ὧν εἶχον ἕκαστα.—XEN. *Anab.* iv. 5. 6.

(*b*) A Partitive Genitive is not unfrequently used in Greek without any governing word (compare the French use of *du, des*).

22. The Objective Genitive is added to Substantives and Adjectives, derived from transitive verbs, or containing a transitive idea, and corresponds to the object which the verb itself would govern ; τούτων ἴδρις, 'acquainted with these things.'

23. The same Genitive is added to all words which imply a physical or mental aim, and to express the object of a sensation or a desire ; ἥμαρτε τοῦ σκόπου, 'he missed the mark ;' ἐπὶ Κρήτης, 'in the direction of Crete.'

Obs.—Verbs of hearing and learning often take a genitive of the person and an accusative of the thing heard ; ταῦτά σου ἤκουσα, 'I heard this from you.'

24. The Genitive of Ablation is joined to words which imply origin, separation, hindering, depriving, and differing : διεῖχον ἀλλήλων, 'they were distant from each other ;' Δαρείου καὶ Παρυσάτιδος γίγνονται παῖδες δύο, 'of Darius and Parysatis two sons were born.'—XEN. *Anab.* i. 1. 1.

25. The Genitive of Relation or Reference is added to comparatives and to words implying superiority or inferiority, dominion and submission : ἀμείνων τοῦ πατρός, 'better than his father ;' τῆς χώρας ἄρχειν, 'to rule over the province.'   Also to some adverbs of relative position, as εἴσω τῆς τάφρου, 'within the trench.'

45

(*a*) To this head belong the Genitives of Price and Measure : πολλοῦ ἄξιος, 'of great value ;' ποταμὸς εὖρος πλέθρου, 'a river one hundred feet wide.'

26. The same Genitive is added to many adjectives and adverbs and interjections, to point out the person or thing to which they refer. It may often be translated by 'in' or 'in respect of,' *e.g.* τέλειος τῆς ἀρετῆς, 'perfect in virtue,' οἴμοι τῆς τύχης, 'woe is me for my fortune.'

(*a*) It is also added to verbs and adjectives which imply fulness and plenty or their opposites (sometimes called the Genitive of Material) : πλήρης ἰχθύων, 'full of fish.'

(*b*) And to words of accusing, condemning, and acquitting, and of praise and blame, to denote the matter of the charge or commendation : φόνου διώκειν, 'to prosecute for murder.'

27. The Genitive case with the participle (the Genitive Absolute) is used to indicate the circumstances under which an action takes place, or which limit it, and may therefore be classed under this head.

28. Time, and sometimes space, within which, is put in the Genitive case, as τῆς ἐπιούσης νυκτός, 'at some point in the following night;' τὴν ἐπιοῦσαν νύκτα, 'for the whole of the following night.'

The Verb Infinite.

29. The Infinitive is the noun-form of the verb, and is inflected by prefixing to it the different cases of the neuter article τό. Its oblique cases, when thus inflected, may be governed by prepositions, and may follow most of the constructions which belong to the case. It governs the same cases as the verb finite.

It is used—

(*a*) As Subject or Object to another verb, or as Predicate with a copulative verb : ἐξῆν μένειν, 'it was in their power to stay;' αἱροῦνται πολεμεῖν, 'they choose war.'

(*b*) Obliquely, with an accusative of its subject (§ 43).

(*c*) Prolatively, in order to define more completely the words to which it is joined. In this sense it corresponds to the use of the Accusative (§ 13): δεινὸς λέγειν, 'skilled in speaking.'

(*d*) Explanatorily, as ἐπέτρεψε τὴν χώραν διαρπάσαι, 'he gave up the country to them to plunder.' This is really consecutive (§ 49).

(*e*) In a limiting sense in a few idiomatic expressions, as ὡς εἰπεῖν, 'so to speak ;' ἑκὼν εἶναι, 'if one can help it.'

30. Not only the Infinitive, but the Infinitive with its subject, object, and all its limiting words or phrases, may be preceded by the article τό, and the whole treated as a single noun : τὸ δι' ἡμᾶς Πελοποννησίους αὐτοῖς μὴ βοηθῆσαι παρέσχεν ὑμῖν Σαμίων κόλασιν, 'the fact that we prevented the Peloponnesians from coming to their aid left you free to chastise the Samians.'—THUC. i. 41.

31. The place of the Latin Gerundive is supplied by the verbal adjective in -τέος, which is followed by a Dative of the agent.

> (*a*) The Gerundive of intransitive verbs is only used impersonally, and is followed by the genitive or dative, when the verb requires those cases : ἐπιχειρητέον τῷ ἔργῳ, 'one must attempt the task.'
>
> (*b*) Similarly the Gerundive of transitive verbs is used impersonally and followed by the accusative : οἰστέον τὴν τύχην, 'one must bear one's lot.'

The Tenses.

32. The Present Tense-Stem denotes continuous or repeated action.

Hence the Present and Imperfect tenses of the Indicative are used when an action is or was going on, or incomplete, or habitual : γράφει, 'he is writing ;' ἔκτεινόν με, 'they were killing me,' or 'they tried to kill me.'

In the other moods it denotes that the action is continued and not momentary.

> (*a*) In the Indicative, the Present is used as in Latin, as a graphic historic tense, and has historic sequences (37 *a*).

33. The Aorist-Stem denotes the simple action of the verb. In the Indicative mood it is only used of definite actions in *past* time ; in the other moods it denotes the action as a single whole, without reference to its continuance. So νοσεῖν is 'to be sick,' νοσῆσαι 'to fall sick ;' θνήσκειν 'to be on one's deathbed,' θανεῖν 'to die.'

But where the Optative or Infinitive, or the Participle of the Aorist, in indirect discourse, or the Participle as the equivalent of a Causal or Temporal Clause (§ 58), represents an original Indicative, it denotes the simple occurrence of an action which is past relatively to the leading verb, as ἀπῆλθεν ἀτιμασθείς, 'he went away after being disgraced.'

> (*a*) A single instance of a repeated action is taken as a specimen of what has happened and may happen again, and so the Aorist is used to express that which past experience shows to happen frequently (the Frequentative Aorist). In this case it may be translated by the English present or by 'is wont to be.'
>
> (*b*) The Imperative of the Aorist is not used in prohibitions in the second person, its place being supplied by the Subjunctive.

34. The Perfect-stem denotes the completed action, or, more strictly, the state resulting from the completed action, *e.g.* κτάομαι, 'I earn ;' κέκτημαι, 'I possess ;' βουλεύομαι, 'I deliberate ;' βεβούλευμαι, 'I have made up my mind.'

35. The Future implies not only future time, but also purpose and intention. There is no Future tense in the Subjunctive Mood, which itself implies a reference to the future, and the Future Optative is only used to represent the Future Indicative in sentences actually or virtually oblique.

(*a*) There are in the passive voice two Futures.

    (1) The Future of the single act formed from the Aorist stem (λυθήσομαι).

    (2) The Future of the completed act, formed from the Perfect stem (λελύσομαι) ; which is used sometimes to denote a sudden or immediate result. *Cf.* XEN. *Anab.* i. 5. 16, νομίζετε ἐν τῇδε τῇ ἡμέρᾳ ἐμέ κατακεκόψεσθαι, 'I shall be cut down, my fate will be settled, that very day.' This Future is formed in the active voice by the perfect participle with ἔσομαι.

The Moods.

36. There are in Greek four moods, the Indicative, the Imperative, the Subjunctive, and the Optative.

The Indicative states a thing as plain fact; the Imperative expresses direct commands; the Subjunctive and Optative are mostly used in Subordinate Clauses to express a state or action which is contingent or dependent upon some other state or action.

• **37.** The Subjunctive refers to present or future time ; the Optative is based upon circumstances either past or merely imagined as possible.

    (*a*) Hence the Subjunctive follows those tenses which refer to present time (called principal or *primary* tenses). The Optative follows those which refer to the past time, or *historic* tenses. (Note that the Subjunctive has *primary*, the Optative *historic* endings, and that the Imperative always implies primary time. What is sequence of *tenses* in Latin is sequence of *moods* in Greek.)

38. Hence also, in suppositions the Subjunctive denotes that which is practical, and will soon be settled one way or another : ἐὰν ἔχω, 'if I have, which I shall soon know ;' the Optative that which is merely possible or conceivable : εἰ ἔχοιμι, 'were I to have, as I may possibly.'

39. The Subjunctive is used—

    (*a*) Independently in simple questions to express doubt or deliberation, ποῦ στῶ; 'where am I to stand?' and in the first person in exhortations and commands. This Subjunctive is retained in a dependent clause in primary sequence, but is changed into the Optative when the question becomes dependent upon a past tense, as οὐκ ᾔδειν ποῦ σταίην, 'I did not know where to stand.'

    (*b*) Dependently, with relative and conditional particles, generally followed by ἄν, to put a general case, after primary time : ὃς ἂν ταῦτα ποιῇ, 'whoever does this ;' ἐὰν ταῦτα γένηται, 'if ever this happens.'

40. The Optative is used—

    (*a*) Independently, to express a wish that may be realised.

48

(*b*) Dependently, to express frequency, and to generalise after past time, and so especially after the imperfect : εἰ μὲν ἐντύχοιέν τισι κρείσσους ὄντες τῶν πολεμίων διέφευγον αὐτούς, 'if (= whenever) they met any of the enemy, though they were stronger than they, they constantly fled from them.'—THUC. vii. 44.

The Voices.

41. There are three Voices in Greek, the Active, the Middle, and the Passive.

(*a*) The Active and Passive are used much as in Latin, the Greek equivalent of *a* or *ab* with the ablative of the agent being ὑπό with the genitive.

(*b*) The Middle Voice, which was probably the earliest form of the Passive, is used of *reflexive* action ; *i.e.* of action which comes back to the agent, either (1) as interested in the action, *i.e.* as recipient, or (2) as getting the action done, or (3) as having it reciprocated by another.

Exx.—(1) μεταπέμπεσθαί τινα, 'to send for a person' (to come to one) ; (2) διδάσκεσθαι τὸν υἱόν, 'to have one's son taught ;' (3) διαλύεσθαι πόλεμον, 'to put an end to a war by mutual treaty ;' διαλέγεσθαι (which consequently is only used in the middle) 'to converse.'

Obs.—The same remark applies to those words which take a middle form for the future, the agent's will being more involved in the future than in the other tenses ; as ἀκούσομαι, 'I will hear.'

The Compound Sentence.

42. A Compound Sentence consists of two or more Simple Sentences connected together, of which one is the principal, the others are subordinate.

Subordinate Sentences are of three kinds, corresponding to the parts of speech whose place they fill in the principal sentence, viz., Substantival, Adjectival, and Adverbial.

Substantival Clauses (*L. P.* p. 141).

43. *Oblique enuntiation* is expressed—

(*a*) By the Infinitive, with the accusative of the subject, when it is different from the subject of the principal sentence, but with the nominative when it is the same (see Rule 9), the Future being used after words of promising : ἔφη Νικίαν στρατηγεῖν, 'he said that Nicias was general.'   49

By this construction it is possible at any moment to show that the words or thoughts are not the writer's own, without the use of any introductory phrases such as 'he said,' 'he replied.'

> *Obs.*—But with words like λέγεται, δοκεῖ, etc., the personal construction is preferred, *e.g.* λέγεται Ἀπόλλων ἐκδεῖραι Μαρσύαν, 'it is said that Apollo flayed Marsyas.'

(*b*) By ὡς or ὅτι, with the Indicative after primary tenses, and with the Optative after historic tenses, after verbs of saying and knowing. ὅτι generally introduces an actual fact, ὡς the speaker's impression or representation ōf it. *N.B.* Note that the Subjunctive is never used in oblique narration or interrogation unless it represents in primary sequence a Subjunctive in the direct.

(*c*) By a Participle agreeing with the object, after verbs of knowledge and perception. The nominative is preserved if the participle is predicated of the subject of the principal verb. οἱ Ἕλληνες οὐκ ᾔδεσαν Κῦρον τεθνηκότα, 'the Greeks did not know that Cyrus was dead;' Ἴσθι ἀνόητος ὤν, 'be sure that you lack common sense.'

(*d*) By the Indicative of past or present time, or the Subjunctive or Optative, according to the tense of the principal verb, of future time, with μή, after verbs of fearing : φοβοῦμαι μὴ τοῦτο γέγονε, 'I fear that this has happened ;'—μὴ γένηται, 'that it may happen ;' ἐφοβούμην μὴ γένοιτο. (This is partly final.)

44. *Oblique Petition* is expressed by the Accusative and Infinitive, or the Infinitive alone.

45. *Oblique Interrogation* is expressed by the Indicative after primary, and the Optative after historic tenses, following an interrogative pronoun or particle, direct or oblique (*e.g.* τίς or ὅστις) or the conjunction εἰ, dependent on a verb of asking, doubting, telling, etc.

46. The Indicative, and the Subjunctive, with or without ἄν, of Subordinate clauses, are preserved in oratio obliqua after primary tenses, but are changed into the Optative without ἄν after historic tenses.

47. In oblique enuntiation and interrogation the moods and tenses of the original direct sentence are often retained, in order to approach more closely to the words of the speaker. (Graphic Sequence.)

Adjectival Clauses.

48. Adjectival Clauses are introduced by the Relative ὅς or one of its particles, which is followed by the Indicative when it defines an individual by definite actions or qualities ; by the Subjunctive with ἄν after Primary, or by the Optative without ἄν after Historic tenses, when it defines a class, or implies a condition.

The relative ὅς, like the Latin *qui* (L. P. § 150), but more rarely, expresses purpose, consequence, or cause. See §§ 49, 50 *c*, 51.

50.

49. *Consecutive Clauses* denote the result of an action, and are introduced—

    (*a*) By ὥστε, which is followed by the Accusative and Infinitive, or the simple Infinitive if the subject is unchanged, when the result is indicated as *natural*, whether it really follows or not ; by the Indicative when attention is called to the fact that it does *actually* follow ; as, ἤλαυνον ἐπὶ τοὺς Μένωνος, ὥστε ἐκείνους ἐκπεπλῆχθαι (XEN. *Anab.* i. 5. 13), 'they charged Menon's soldiers, so that they were thrown into a panic,' where the result follows, but no special attention is called to the fact ; the charge was sufficient to scare them: οὐχ ἧκεν ὁ Τισσαφέρνης, ὥστε ἐφρόντιζον (*Ibid.* ii. 3. 25), where Tissaphernes' absence was not only enough to make them think, but did make them think, etc.

In the same way οἷος, ὅσος, are followed by the Infinitive, as οὐκ ἔστιν οἷος ταῦτα ποιεῖν, 'he is not the man to do this.'

ὥστε is also used (as well as ἐφ' ᾧ, ἐφ' ᾧτε) with the Infinitive, to denote the condition or understanding on which a thing is done, as συμμαχίαν ἐποιήσαντο, ὥστε μὴ στρατεύειν, 'on condition that they should not be required to serve.' (See § 30.)

    (*b*) by the Relative ὅς, or ὅστις, or one of its particles, as τίς οὕτως εὐήθης ὅστις ἀγνοεῖ, 'who is so simple as not to know?'

    Obs.—In the former case Xenophon often uses the simple ὡς for ὥστε. The negatives are οὐ with the Indicative, μή with the Infinitive.

50. *Final Clauses* denote purpose, and are introduced by ἵνα, ὡς, ὅπως, μή, ἵνα μή, ὡς μή, ὅπως μή, followed by the Subjunctive or the Optative, according as the verb on which they depend is in primary or historic time.

    (*a*) Purpose is also expressed as in Latin by the Future Participle, and by the Accusative of the Gerund with the preposition.

    (*b*) Also by the simple Infinitive after verbs of giving, going, and the like, as οἶνον ἔδωκα πιεῖν, 'I gave him wine to drink.'

    (*c*) The Relative ὅς or ὅστις, when it expresses purpose, is followed by the Future Indicative, *never* by the Subjunctive : ἡγεμόνα αἰτεῖν, ὅστις ἀπάξει, 'to lead them back.'—XEN. *Anab.* i. 3. 14.

    (*d*) A purpose which is beyond attainment because some necessary condition is unfulfilled (Eng. 'that I might have been'), is expressed by a past tense of the Indicative with ἵνα, ὡς, or ὅπως.

    (*e*) Verbs of precaution and consideration are followed by ὅπως or ὅπως μή with the Future Indicative after *primary*, or the Optative after *historic* tenses ; ἐπιμελοῦνται ὅπως μὴ τοιοῦτοι ἔσονται.—XEN. *Cyr.* i. 2. 3.

By the omission of ὅρα or σκόπει this becomes hortative : ὅπως ἔσεσθε ἄνδρες, 'see ye be men.'—XEN. *Anab.* i. 7. 3.

51. *Causal Clauses* are introduced by ὅτι and διότι, sometimes by ὡς, ἐπεί, or ἐπειδή, followed by the Indicative, the former explaining a fact, the latter connecting cause and effect, or by ὅς, ὅς γε, ὅστις, with the Indicative: ἐπεὶ ὑμεῖς ἐμοὶ οὐ θέλετε πείθεσθαι, ἐγὼ σὺν ὑμῖν ἕψομαι, 'since you will not obey me, I will accompany you' (XEN. *Anab.* i. 3. 6). Κλέαρχον παρεκάλεσε σύμβουλον, ὅς γε ἐδόκει προτιμηθῆναι μάλιστα τῶν Ἑλλήνων, 'he called Clearchus to his counsel, since he seemed to be the most distinguished of the Greeks.' (Negative οὐ.)

52. *Temporal Clauses* are introduced by ὅτε, ὁπότε, ἡνίκα, ὡς (when), ἕως, ἔστε, ἐν ᾧ (whilst, as long as), πρίν (before), ἕως, ἔστε, μέχρις οὗ (until), ἐπεί, ἐπειδή (after), followed by the Indicative to express a certain known and definite time, past, present, or future ; by ἄν with the Subjunctive, after Primary tenses to express present or future time of uncertain or repeated acts (whenever) ; and by the Optative after Historic tenses of uncertain or repeated acts.

(a) πρίν, πρὶν ἤ, and πρότερον ἤ are generally followed by the Infinitive after affirmations, unless it is wished to denote that the fact took place, when the Indicative is used.

(b) πρὶν ἄν and sometimes πρίν with the Subjunctive, and πρίν with the Optative, are used only in sentences actually or virtually negative. οὐ χρή με ἀπελθεῖν, πρὶν ἄν δῶ δίκην, 'you must not let me go, till I have suffered for it' (XEN. *Anab.* v. 7. 5) ; οὐδαμόθεν ἀφίεσαν, πρὶν παραθεῖεν ἄριστον, 'they would not let them go, till they had served them with breakfast' (iv. 5. 30).

(c) ἕως with the Aorist = until, with the Present = as long as.

53. *Conditional Clauses* (L. P., p. 144), are introduced by εἰ, ἐάν, εἴπερ, followed by μή if the sentence be negative. Four classes are distinguished :—

(a) *Pure condition :* where the question is one of fact and the consequence follows if the fact be granted (sumptio Dati) ; the Indicative is used in both Protasis and Apodosis ; εἴ τι ἁμαρτάνεις ἀλγεῖς, *si quid peccas, doles.*

(b) *Practical supposition :* where the condition is a supposition, but one which has a speedy prospect of decision, and the consequence is certain to follow on the fulfilment of the condition (sumptio Dandi) ; by ἐάν or ἤν with the Subjunctive in the Protasis, with the Future of the Indicative in the Apodosis, ἐάν τι ἁμάρτῃς ἀλγήσει, *si quid peccaveris, dolebis.* ἐάν is often used in a frequentative sense = if ever.

(c) *Possible Supposition :* where the condition and consequence are both hypothetical without any suggestion of their being more than possible and conceivable (sumptio Ficti) ; the Optative is used with εἰ in the Protasis, and the Optative with ἄν (which connects it with its conditions) in the Apodosis, as εἴ τι ἁμαρτάνοις, ἀλγοίης ἄν, *si quid pecces, doleas.*

52

Note.—In (*b*) and (*c*) the place of the Protasis is often filled by a relative clause where ὄς or ὄστις = εἴ τις.

(*d*) *Impossible Supposition :* where the condition, being a *supposition* contrary to actual fact, can no longer be fulfilled, and the consequence is therefore impossible; a past tense of the Indicative in the Protasis followed by a past tense of the Indicative with ἀν, the imperfect denoting continuance, the aorist the single act, εἴ τι ἡμάρτανες ἤλγεις ἀν, *si quid peccares, doleres.*

(*e*) Conditional sentences of various shades of meaning are formed by combining the Protasis of one of these principal forms with the Apodosis of another; *e.g.* εἰ γὰρ οὗτοι ὀρθῶς ἀπέστησαν, ὑμεῖς ἀν οὐ χρεὼν ἄρχοιτε. The real condition is contained in ὀρθῶς, 'if it should turn out that they were right in their revolt, then you will be holding an unjustifiable rule.' The particular case carries a principle which proves a general conclusion.

Obs.—In particular, an indefinite case in past time (εἰ with Optative= if ever) is followed by a past tense of the Indicative with ἀν to denote what actually followed in each case (ἀν, where the condition is fulfilled).

·54. From classes (*c*) (*d*) of Conditional sentences arise some abbreviated forms :—

(*a*) The Apodosis being suppressed, the Protasis alone expresses a strong wish, like our 'if only,' or the Latin *O si ;* εἰ ἔχοιμι, 'if only I might have' (a wish possible to be realised); εἰ ἠδυνήθην, 'I wish I had been able ' (impossible).

(*b*) The suppression of the Protasis in (*c*) leaves the Apodosis to express a contingent futurity ; ποιοίην ἀν, 'I will do —— if the necessary circumstances ever arise.' In the second person it is used to express a courteous request, δέχοιο ἀν, 'please accept it,' —*i.e.* 'you will accept it if you wish to oblige.'

55. In oratio obliqua, the Indicative or Optative of the Apodosis is represented by the Infinitive or the Participle (§ 43 *c*), the ἀν being retained.

(*a*) The Apodosis can also be put, if necessary, into a participial form, generally with ὡς.

56. *Concessive* or *Limitative Clauses* are formed by εἰ καί or καί εἰ with the indicative or optative, or by ἐάν καί with the subjunctive, after Primary tenses (negative μή), but more generally by participles with the particle καίπερ prefixed (negative οὐ).

57. *Comparative Clauses*, comparing with actual fact, are expressed by ὡς with the indicative, except in the oblique ; comparing with a supposition (Latin *quasi*), by ὡσεί with the construction of the Conditional Sentence. A noticeable form of the first is ὡς ἠδύνατο, 'to his power ;' with the superlative ἠδύνατο is often omitted : as, ὡς πλεῖστοι, 'the greatest number possible.'

The Participle.

58. Several of the above clauses may be represented by participles, as :—

(*a*) *Causal*, sometimes with ἅτε or ὡς, as, νομίζων ἀμείνονας εἶναι ὑμᾶς προσέλαβον, 'I took you with me, because I thought you to be better than they were.'

(*b*) *Temporal*, the present participle expressing simultaneous time, the aorist prior time, and the future future, as compared with the leading verb, as ἡδὺ σωθέντα μεμνῆσθαι πόνων where σωθέντα = ἐπειδὰν σωθῇ τις.

(*c*) *Conditional*, as ἁμαρτάνων ἀλγεῖς, ἀλγήσει, ἀλγοίης ἄν, ἤλγεις ἄν ; in negative sentences the use of μή marks the participle as conditional.

(*d*) *Concessive*, with or without καί or καίπερ, ὅμως being often added in the Apodosis ; καίπερ εἰδότες, 'although they know.'

(*e*) *Comparative*, with ὡς.

(*f*) The Participle is also used instead of another verb to express the means or the circumstances which lead up to or attend the verb, ταῦτα ποιήσας ἀπώλεσε τὴν ἀρχήν, 'by doing this he lost his empire.' This is called the Modal use. (*Cp.* § 27.)

59. The Participle is used in Greek with several verbs expressing existence, as, τυγχάνειν, ἄρχεσθαι (to begin), λανθάνειν, φαίνεσθαι, or joy or sorrow, as χαίρειν, λυπεῖσθαι, and with φθάνειν, to be beforehand, παύειν, to stop, and with the adjectives δῆλος and φανερός.

Note.—φαίνομαι ὤν = I plainly am ; φαίνομαι εἶναι = I appear to be.

60. The Participle is used predicatively with the definite noun (§ 5), where we use a verbal substantive, as ἅμα τῷ σίτῳ ἀκμάζοντι, 'with the ripening of the corn.'

61. The Accusative of the Participle of impersonal verbs, or verbs used impersonally, is used absolutely, as δέον, since it is necessary, δόξαν, when it had been resolved.

The Negatives.

62. There are two Negatives, οὐ and μή ; οὐ appears in negative statements, μή in negative conceptions, such as purpose, condition, consequence.

(*a*) μή is consequently used in prohibitions, direct and oblique, in oblique sentences after verbs of swearing and pledging, in conditions, and in deliberative, final, and consecutive clauses where the result is not represented as actually achieved.

(*b*) μή is used with the relative and also with adjectives and participles with the article, when the relative or article denotes a class, as ὁ μὴ ἀδικῶν, or ὃς μὴ ἀδικεῖ, 'whoever is not dishonest.' ἃ ἂν μὴ δράσῃς, 'whatever you do not do.'

63. The Negative in oblique enunciation is often attached to the introductory verb, as οὔ φημι='nego;' οὐκ ἐῶ, 'I forbid;' so οὐκ ἀξιῶ τοῦτο ποιεῖν, 'I think I ought not to do this.'

64. The Negative in Greek is repeated with each thing denied, as οὔποτε οὐδεὶς οὐδαμοῦ ταῦτα ἐποίησε, 'no one ever did this under any circumstances.' If the verb comes at the beginning it has its own negative, as οὐκ ἐποίησε ταῦτα οὐδείς, 'no one did this.' Otherwise, two negatives make an affirmative, as οὐδεὶς οὐ ταῦτα ἐποίησε = 'everybody did this.'

65. The Negative μὴ is inserted before the infinitive after verbs of denying, hindering, forbidding, to make the subordinate clause carry its own full meaning : κωλύω σε μὴ ταῦτα δρᾶν, 'I prevent you from doing this.'

> (a) An infinitive which for any reason has μὴ, takes the double negative μὴ οὐ, when it follows an actual or virtual negative, as, οὐ κωλύω σε μὴ οὐ ταῦτα δρᾶν. So ἀδύνατα ἦν μὴ οὐ μεγάλα βλάπτειν, THUC.; ὥστε αἰσχύνην εἶναι μὴ οὐ συσπουδάζειν, XEN. *Anab.* ii. 3.11.

The Prepositions.

66. The meaning of Prepositions in Greek is modified by the use of the cases to which they are attached, the Genitive implying separation, or motion from, or aim; the Dative, attachment to, or rest at; the Accusative, motion along or towards; *e.g.* παρά (= alongside) with the Genitive means ' from (the side of),' with the Dative 'at the side of,' with the Accusative 'along' or 'to the side of;' μετά (our 'mid') with the Genitive is ' from the middle of' and so in company ' with ;' with the Dative, 'among,' and with the Accusative, 'along the middle of,' or 'to the midst of,' and so, as one who goes to join a party follows it, 'after,' 'in pursuit of.'

67. The following prepositions take one case only :—
> (a) The Genitive, πρό, ἀπό, ἐκ or ἐξ, ἀντί, πλήν, ἄνευ, πέραν, μεταξύ, ἕνεκα (which is sometimes put after its case).
> (b) The Dative, ἐν and σύν.
> (c) The Accusative, εἰς, ὡς (with persons only), and ἀνά.

68. The following take two cases, the Genitive and Accusative: διά, κατά, and ὑπέρ.

69. The following take the Genitive, Dative, and Accusative :—ἀμφί, περί, παρά, πρός, ἐπί, ὑπό, μετά.

THE USES OF THE

SUBJUNCTIVE AND OPTATIVE.

I.

In Principal Clauses.

1. WISH or COMMAND.
 (*a*) First person plural, ἴωμεν, 'let us go.'
 (*b*) Aorist with μή in prohibitions, τοῦτο μὴ δράσῃς, 'do not do this.'

2. DELIBERATIVE, in direct questions (or indirect in *primary* sequence).
 ποῖ ἴωμεν; 'Whither are we to go?' (οὐκ ἔχουσι ποῖ ἴωσι.)

3. With οὐ μή (with the aorist) a strong DENIAL (probably an elliptical case of II. 1).
 οὐ μὴ ἔλθῃ, 'there is no chance of his coming.'

1. WISH.—The pure Optative to express a wish of possible fulfilment.
 εὐτυχοίης, 'may you prosper.'
 (Negative μή.)

2. POTENTIAL or CONDITIONAL. With ἄν, especially in the apodosis of conditional sentences, with εἰ and the optative in the protasis.
 (Negative οὐ.)

II.

In Governed Clauses.

1. FINAL, in *primary* sequence, to express purpose, or after verbs of precaution and fear.
 (Negative μή.)

2. INDEFINITE, after relative pronouns and particles, and hypothetical conjunctions, generally with ἄν, to express indefiniteness in *primary* time. (Negative μή.)

Note.—The subjunctive is never used to make a statement, except in I. 3.; and never represents any other mood than its own in oblique statements or questions.

1. FINAL, in *historic* sequence.
 (Negative μή.)

2. INDEFINITE, after relative pronouns, and in *historic* time, *without* ἄν. (Negative μή.)

3. INDIRECT QUESTIONS, in *historic* sequence. (Negative οὐ.)

4. INDIRECT STATEMENT, after ὡς and ὅτι in *historic* sequence.
 (Negative οὐ.)

5. CONDITIONAL,—With εἰ to express possible but unpractical hypotheses. (Negative μή.)

6. INDIRECT DELIBERATIVE (οὐκ εἶχον ποῖ ἴοιεν). (Negative μή.)

NOTES.

CHAPTER I.

1. ὅτι ... διὰ τοῦτο.] This inversion makes the reason more emphatic.

οὐδὲ μειόνων ἂν τυγχάνοι ἐπαίνων] It were unjust that a man should not receive any praise, even though it came short of his deserts. The ἄν, which some editors omit, seems necessary to explain οὐδὲ, after εἰ. The protasis to οὐκ ἂν καλῶς ἔχοι itself contains another condition.

2. τοῖς προγόνοις ὀνομαζομένοις] When his ancestors are enumerated, or, in the recounting of his pedigree; a kind of instrumental or modal dative. Compare XENOPHON's *Anabasis*, vi. 1. 10 : Ξενοφῶντι δὲ διὰ τῆς μεσογαίας πορευομένῳ (= during Xenophon's progress) οἱ ἱππεῖς προκαταθέοντες ἐντυγχάνουσι πρεσβευταῖς πορευομένοις ποι.

ὁπόστος κ.τ.λ.] How many generations he was removed from Herakles. The Spartan kings traced their pedigree up to Aristodemus, one of the great-grandsons of Hyllus, the son of Herakles, who with his brothers Temenus and Kresphontes led the migration of the Dorians into the Peloponnesus, known in legendary history as the 'return of the Heracleidae.' Aristodemus was killed before the expedition started, and left twin sons Eurysthenes and Prokles, who in the final distribution of the conquered land received by lot their father's portion, Sparta. In this way the legend accounts for the fact that there were always two kings at Sparta.

τούτοις] In apposition with τοῖς προγόνοις.

3. ταύτῃ] On this count.

βασιλεύουσι μὲν κ.τ.λ] Although they are kings, it is only of an ordinary city, ἐπιτυχούσης, such as you come across every day, and so, unimportant.

δευτέρων] Second-rate.

ἡγεμόνων] At the time when Xenophon wrote (about 360 B.C.) the death of Epaminondas had practically left the supremacy (ἡγεμονία) to Sparta once more. In the early times and during the Persian

E

wars, and again for a time after the downfall of Athens at the end of the Peloponnesian war, it had been the leading state in Greece.

4. It was their great merit that they never used their power so as to stir the jealousy of the people, and never grasped at greater power than the terms of their original investiture allowed them.

ἄλλη μὲν—αὕτη δέ] Whereas . . . this.

τυραννίς] Absolute monarchy won by force; βασιλεία, in the later times, constitutional monarchy. The kings of Sparta were kept under considerable checks, and their political power had before this become insignificant, save where, as in Agesilaus, personal strength of character asserted it. They had, however, many important privileges, and were always looked up to with great respect, as the representatives of the founder's house, and the religious heads of the nation. (Compare the ἄρχων βασιλεὺς at Athens, and the 'rex sacrificulus' at Rome.)

συνεχὴς βασιλεία] An uninterrupted monarchy.

5. ὡς ὄντος] Claiming to be.

ἀνεπικλητότερον] More unimpeachable.

κριθέντα] Translate 'when a man has been judged . . . what further proof is needed?' Mark the literal construction: τὸ . . . ἀξιωθῆναι is the subject.

King Agis died in 399 B.C. Lysander, who had been commander of the fleet, and conqueror of Athens, puffed up by his success, and urged on by the flatteries of his friends, had intrigued to get himself made king, and to make the royal office not hereditary, but elective. Having failed in his attempt, he thought to advance himself in another way by getting his friend Agesilaus, who was a younger half-brother of the late king, put on the throne in the place of Agis' son. At his prompting Agesilaus contested the legitimacy of Leotychides and claimed the sceptre for himself. Some doubts had been expressed as to Leotychides' birth, but, doubtless, what decided the question in his uncle's favour was that he was but a lad of fifteen, while Agesilaus was a mature man of forty. Objection was taken to him because he was lame, but Lysander, by an ingenious interpretation of an oracle, managed to carry the day in his favour. [XEN. *Hellen.* iii. 3. 3 : ὡς οὐκ οἴοιτο τὸν θεὸν τοῦτο κελεύειν φυλάξασθαι, μὴ προσπταίσας τις χωλεύσῃ (physical lameness), ἀλλὰ μᾶλλον μὴ οὐκ ὢν τοῦ γένους βασιλεύσῃ.]

6. ἔτι νέος ὤν] He was over forty, so the expression seems hardly suitable.

ἐξηγγέλθη κ.τ.λ.] The Persians had not forgiven the Spartans for the help they had given to the younger Cyrus. At the beginning of 398 B.C. Derkyllidas, being appointed commander of the Greeks, had made a truce with Tissaphernes in order to attack Pharnabazus. In the following year he was commanded by the Ephors to attack Tissaphernes in Caria, and the fleet under Pharax was ordered to co-operate with him. The two satraps joined their forces, so that Derkyllidas could effect but little, and an armistice was concluded (397 B.C.). Pharnabazus availed himself of it to make extensive preparations for a fresh war. He got down Persian troops, and began to raise a fleet of 300 sail in Phoenicia and Cilicia to be placed under the command of the Athenian admiral Conon.

7. **ἐὰν δῶσιν**] The graphic sequence, the original mood being preserved. *Syntax*, § 47.

τριάκοντα Σπαρτιατῶν] As a sort of council of officers (ἡγεμόνας καὶ συμβούλους, PLUTARCH, c. vi.). Spartan citizens did not, as a rule, go as soldiers on foreign service.

νεοδαμώδεις] Enfranchised Helots, who had received their freedom as a reward for their bravery in war. σύνταγμα, a corps.

βούληται] Is bent upon.

ἀσχολίαν παρέξειν] He would keep him too busy to invade Greece.

8. **αὐτὸ τοῦτο**] The mere fact of desiring. The accusative of the thing alone with ἄγαμαι is rare, but is used by Xenophon, *Cyrop.* ii. 3. 19.

πρόσθεν] Under Darius and Xerxes.

ἐπιόντα κ.τ.λ.] To carry on an offensive rather than a defensive warfare. Some word like τινὰ is understood as the subject of the infinitive. Similarly with δαπανῶντα (acc. sing.), and πολεμεῖν.

δαπανῶντα] By obtaining his supplies from the people among whom he was. Trans. 'at his expense, and not at that of the Greeks.'

μὴ περὶ τῆς Ἑλλάδος] To let the stake be the possession, not of Greece, but of Asia.

9. **ὡς ἐστρατήγησεν**] What sort of a general he was.

10. **ἥδε πρώτη πρᾶξις**] This was his first performance. πρώτη πρᾶξις is predicate, or it would have the article.

Τισσαφέρνης ὤμοσεν] The armistice was renewed for three months, in order to allow time for communication with the Persian court. Derkyllidas had demanded the independence of the Greek cities in Asia, and envoys had been sent to negotiate these terms.

Tissaphernes told Agesilaus that he hoped that they would be granted, and with this understanding swore to the armistice, *Hellen.* iii. 4. 5, 6.

οὓς πέμψειε] Whom he had sent.

πόλεις ῾Ελληνίδας] Treated apparently as one word : generally τὰς ῾Ελληνίδας πόλεις, or, τὰς πόλεις τὰς ῾Ελληνίδας.

ὁρισάμενος τρεῖς μῆνας] Having limited the time allowed for the negotiations to three months.

11. εἰρήνην πράττειν] Promoting a peace: so *Hellen.* iv. 4. 7. ἔπραττε τὴν εἴσοδον, he was trying to get an entrance.

12. ἐπίορκον belongs to ἐμφανίσας, ἄπιστον to ἐποίησεν.

μὴ ψευδόμενον] μὴ, with the participle, represents it as depending on the mind of the subject of the leading verb. Translate 'not one to break compacts.'

ἐποίησε συντίθεσθαι] Often explained as a consecutive infinitive without ὥστε, but it seems better to take πάντας συντίθεσθαι as object to ἐποίησε. 'He made them enter into compacts with him without hesitation.'

μέγα φρονήσας ἐπὶ] Presuming upon. The whole of this passage is repeated in the *Hellen.* iii. 4. 11.

13. καταβάντι] It had come down from the inland provinces. So compounds of ἀνά are used of persons going inland (cf. ἀνάβασις), and both ἀνὰ and κατὰ are similarly used of motion from or to the coast line from the sea-side ; καταπλεῖν, to sail into harbour, ἀνάγεσθαι, to put out to sea.

προεῖπεν πόλεμον] This was before the three months of the armistice had expired.

τὴν παροῦσαν δύναμιν ᾿Αγησιλάῳ] Agesilaus' existing force.

φαιδρῷ τῷ προσώπῳ] With cheerfulness in his face.

ἐπιορκήσας] By his perjury.

14. στρατευομένῳ] On his march.

ἀγορὰν παρασκευάζειν] To provide a market, *i.e.* he would pay for the provisions that they brought.

πρὸς αὐτὸν εἰς ῎Εφεσον] We should say, 'to him *at* Ephesus.'

15. ἄφιππος] Impracticable for cavalry. It was rough and mountainous. Agesilaus' message to the Carians was simply meant to put Tissaphernes off the scent, and it was successful. He thought that Agesilaus had a personal grudge against him for his deceit, and so prepared to meet the attack by stationing his cavalry in the great plain of Lydia, through which the Greek troops would have to pass to reach the Carian hills.

τῷ ὄντι] sc. ὁρμήσειν. His real destination was.

οἶκον] NEPOS, *Agesil.* 3: Quod ipsius erant plurima domicilia in Caria. Caria had been his satrapy when Cyrus had Lydia.

Μαιανδροῦ] A river that rises near Celaenae in Phrygia (*Xen. Anab.* i. 2. 7). It flows in a S.W. direction towards Caria, and empties itself into the sea opposite to Miletus. In the plain its course is very winding, and its name has thus become proverbial.

16. ἐπὶ Φρυγίας] Phrygia was the province of Pharnabazus. He had made no preparation for the attack, and Tissaphernes brought him no help, so that Agesilaus met with little or no resistance, and took abundance of plunder and of slaves. So PLUTARCH, ch. 9.

τὰς ἀπαντώσας δυνάμεις] Probably small bands that roamed the country. They were too small to offer resistance. This will account for the number of captives mentioned later.

ἔλαβε] Note the change of tense ; this is a summary of the fruits of the whole expedition.

17. ὅσιόν τε καὶ δίκαιον] Right and fair.

ἐξ ἐκείνου] From that time forward, all being fair in war.

παῖδα] A mere child.

18. ἀντίπροικα] For a mere song ; all but given away.

προεῖπεν] Gave a hint.

ἐπὶ θάλατταν] Where there would be a better market for them.

γραφομένους] They were to make an entry of the price of each thing purchased, and let them have the goods ; not requiring them to pay, that is, till they had sold them again, which they were able to do in the seaports at a considerable profit. The original sale was held on the spot by the λαφυρόπωλαι, whose business it was to receive the proceeds, and to account for them to the public treasury.

οὐδὲν προτελέσαντες] Without advancing anything.

βλάψαντες] The rule was that the spoil should be sold on the spot, so the treasury would not suffer.

19. πρὸς βασιλέα] *i.e.* directly to the king, with whom they would most wish to gain favour ; so ὡς εἰκός.

ὑφηγεῖσθαι] To give information ; put him in the way of treasure.

ταῦτα] Join this with ἁλίσκοιτο.

χρηματίζοιντο] They might be the gainers.

20. πορθουμένη κ.τ.λ.] Note the present participles used of that which is going on.

ἀέναον] Never-failing.

ἐπεμέλετο κ.τ.λ.] If they joined him willingly the land would be οἰκουμένη, but if he conquered them by force it would be πορθουμένη.

21. τοὺς ἁλισκομένους] The captives taken from time to time.

φέρειν = to carry, transport. The children had been sold by their captors to slave-merchants, who abandoned them in their haste to get away from the enemy.

συγκομίζοιντο] Plural, because παιδάρια, though neuter in form, is masculine in sense.

22. τοῖς δ' αὖ κατὰ γῆρας] Some of the prisoners were left behind, as being less vigorous than the others, and so not likely to fetch a great price, and the children were put under their care.

οἱ ἁλισκόμενοι] The old men and the children, who were grateful for their release.

ἀφαιρῶν] Relieving them from the services which are only due from a slave to his master, he enjoined upon them the obedience which free men pay to their rulers.

καὶ τῶν κατὰ κράτος] And fortresses that were impregnable to assault he brought into his power by kindness. The genitive is partitive—some fortresses.

23. οὐδὲ ἐν τῇ Φρυγίᾳ] Not even in Phrygia. He had nearly reached Daskylium, the residence of Pharnabazus, when his small force of cavalry encountered an equal detachment of Persian horse, and was defeated by them. After this defeat, the omens showed themselves unfavourable for any further advance, and he turned off to the sea.—*Hellen.* iii. 4. 13-15.

κατέλεξε] He put on the list. It is followed by the infinitive, because it implies a command.

24. ὅστις] The class mentioned is brought into prominence by this transposing of the relative clause and its grammatical antecedent.

παρέχοιτο] PLUT. *Ages.* ix.: 'Αναχωρήσας εἰς Ἔφεσον ἱππικὸν συνῆγε, τοῖς εὐπόροις προειπών, εἰ μὴ βούλονται στρατεύεσθαι, παρασχεῖν ἕκαστον ἵππον ἀνθ' ἑαυτοῦ καὶ ἄνδρα. The middle here implies that he does it for his own relief.

δόκιμον] One who could pass the inspection (δοκιμασία).

ταῦτα] *plur.* because several things are to be provided.

ὥσπερ ἄν τις κ.τ.λ.] As a man would naturally seek out with eagerness some one to die in his stead. μαστεύω is a poetical word.

πόλεις] viz. those that were specially known for the breeding of horses.

ἱππέας] Those who were to be accepted as substitutes, the ἄνδρες δόκιμοι of the last clause.

εὐθὺς κ.τ.λ.] Would as a matter of course be on their mettle on the score of horsemanship.

κατεσκεύαστο] The tense denotes the rapidity with which an effective force was got together.

ἔαρ] The spring of 395 B.C.

ἥτις] A condensed sentence. For the cavalry squadrons—for the one that showed the best horsemanship. ἥτις with optative represents the ἥτις ἄν of the subjunctive of the proclamation.

σωμάτων] Genitive of reference after ἄριστα ἔχοι; cf. *Hellen.* iv. 5. 15, ὡς τάχους ἕκαστος εἶχε, according to each man's achievements in speed. Translate, 'the one that was most in condition.'

τὰ προσήκοντα] Explained by ἐπὶ στόχον ἰέντας below, as marksmanship.

26. Order—ἐποίησεν δὲ ὅλην τὴν πόλιν ἐν ᾗ ἦν ἀξίαν θέας.

σκυτεῖς, γραφεῖς] The former to cover the shields with leather, the latter to ornament them. They were present in smaller numbers than the smiths and braziers; hence the absence of the article.

πολέμου ἐργαστήριον] A workshop of war, an arsenal-yard.

27. ἐπερρώσθη ἄν] Would have felt in good spirits,—would have been confident of success. The work was so serious and earnest.

'Ἀρτέμιδι] The 'great' Diana of the Ephesians.

28. λῃστῶν] Plundering parties. The captives were brought to Ephesus to be sold as slaves; and Agesilaus directed that when they were put up to auction, they should be exhibited in a state of nudity.

λευκοὺς] The Greeks in their gymnastic exercises were always naked, and so by exposure to the sun were brown and tanned; and in the same way their constant hard training made them tough and muscular; so they looked on these white-skinned and fleshy barbarians as little better than women for their effeminacy. So Plato contrasts τὸν ἐν ἡλίῳ καθαρῷ τεθραμμένον with him that is reared ὑπὸ συμμιγεῖ σκιᾷ, unversed in manly toils and the sweat of labour. —*Phaedr.* p. 239.

μηδὲν διοίσειν ἤ] Would be just the same as.

κράτιστα] According to PLUT. *Ages.* x., Lydia is meant.

ὅπως αὐτόθεν κ.τ.λ.] In order that they might at once begin training themselves in body and mind for the conflict. ὅπως refers to προεῖπε, not to ἡγήσοιτο.

αὐτόθεν] *Lit.* from the spot, and so, immediately, at once.

29. τῷ ὄντι] Really.

δι' ἐρημίας πολεμίων] Through a country where he met no opposition.

30. σκευοφόρων] The baggage-train.

ὁ ἡγεμών] The leader of the Persian horse.

αὐτοί] The cavalry themselves.

31. οὔπω παρείη τὸ πεζόν] It was still in Caria, § 29.

τὰ δέκα ἀφ' ἥβης = τοὺς τὰ δέκα ἀφ' ἥβης ἔτη γεγονότας, *i.e.* the younger hoplites, the men first called out on service, from twenty to thirty years of age. The article τά refers to this classification. They from their youth could reach the enemy sooner.

Note the change of tense in ἐκέλευσε. ἦγεν covers the whole operation ; the aorists mark the details.

ὡς αὐτοῦ τε κ.τ.λ.] As he was following with the whole army.

32. πάντα τὰ δεινά] viz., cavalry and light-armed and hoplites.

ἔπεσον . . . ἔφευγον] Note again the changed tense : the fall was instantaneous, the flight continuous.

ὁ δὲ ᾿Αγησίλαος κ.τ.λ.] While Agesilaus put all his stores together, both what belonged to his friends and what had been taken from the enemy, and enclosed them within his lines.

33. ὡς δὲ ἤκουσε] In thus fortifying his camp, he had anticipated a fresh attack, but now that he finds the enemy disunited, he presses on for the capital.

παρεῖναι] Infinitive of oblique command, implied in κηρύγματι ἐδήλου.

ὡς πρὸς σύμμαχον αὐτόν] Condensed for πρὸς αὐτὸν ὡς πρὸς σύμμαχον.

εἰ δέ τινες κ.τ.λ.] And if any claim Asia for their own, they should come to decide the matter by an appeal to arms with those who are ready to set it free.

34. τὸ ἀπὸ τούτου] From that time forward.

τοὺς μὲν πρόσθεν κ.τ.λ.] Seeing that those who, although they were Greeks, were compelled to do homage, were now honoured by those who had once treated them constantly with insult and outrage. Note the position of ῞Ελληνας, the article not belonging to it, but to ἀναγκαζομένους. Note also the tense of ὑβρίζοντο.

ὑφ' ὧν = ὑπ' ἐκείνων ὑφ' ὧν.

καὶ τὰς τῶν θεῶν τιμάς] προσκυνεῖν implies an abject prostration on the ground, such as is paid to the gods only. The claim to this form of homage has been in modern times, in such countries as China and Burmah, a bar to all diplomatic intercourse with Western nations.

τούτους heightens the contrast.

ἀδῄωτον παρέχων] Guaranteeing it from ravage.

τῷ θεῷ ἐν Δελφοῖς] Delphi was not only the habitation that defined the god, but was also the place of the offering : hence no second article.

ἐν δυοῖν ἐτοῖν] Within two years.

35. κακῶς φέρεσθαι] Prospered ill.

καταπέμψας] Down from Susa.

ἀπέτεμεν] *i.e.* had it cut off—on the legal principle, 'qui facit per alium facit per se.' The people in Sardis complained that Tissaphernes had made no provision for their defence, in his anxiety to protect his own estate in Caria, and the king nòw knew that he had achieved nothing with the large reinforcements that had been sent to him. But there was another and a stronger reason for his fall. Parysatis, the queen-mother, had never forgiven nor forgotten the part that he had taken against her favourite son Cyrus. This was her opportunity. Making the most of these disasters, she induced Artaxerxes to order his death. He was seized in a bath at Colossae, and beheaded.

τὰ μὲν τῶν βαρβάρων κ.τ.λ.] The position of the Asiatics became much more hopeless, and that of Agesilaus more secure. ἐρρωμενέστερα is an irregular comparative of the participle ἐρρωμένος.

ἐπρεσβεύοντο] There came ambassadors.

ἡγεμὼν ἦν] Was at the head of.

36. τὸ ναυτικὸν] Pharax, the Lacedaemonian admiral, with 120 ships, had blockaded Conon, the Athenian, with the Persian fleet, forty in number, in the harbour of Caunus, on the borders of Caria and Lycia. But the Persians sent a relief of forty more sail, and Pharax retired to Rhodes. The Rhodians, however, revolted from Sparta and drove Pharax out of their harbour, which became Conon's main station. Pharax was recalled, and Agesilaus was appointed commander on sea as well as land, so as to secure the co-operation of the two forces. These two functions had hitherto been kept separate : that they were now joined together shows the Spartans' sense of the danger.

τὸ μέγιστον] What is chiefest of all. In apposition with the participial clause that follows.

στρατεύουσαν] Present, with the idea of still existing hostility.

ἦλθεν αὐτῷ βοηθεῖν] When the orders, or the message, came to him to go to his country's aid. Infinitive of oblique command.

οὐδὲν διαφερόντως] Just as if he had been standing in the ephor's court by himself.

ἐπικτήτους] Newly acquired, adscititious. After the events last mentioned, Agesilaus had again invaded the territory of Pharnabazus, and laid waste his residence. This led to an interview in which the two became personal friends, and Agesilaus promised not to war against Pharnabazus as long as there were other

Persians to attack. He had laid his plans accordingly for a great expedition into the interior during the summer of 394 B.C., when he suddenly received a summons home. Tithraustes, the successor of Tissaphernes, after concluding an armistice with Agesilaus, set to work to foment a quarrel in Greece which should lead to the Spartan king's recall. The revolt of Rhodes and the admission of Conon, who was in command of the Persian fleet, was the first spark. Judicious bribes made through a Rhodian named Timocrates brought to a flame the long smouldering jealousy of Sparta which existed already in Thebes and Corinth and Argos. The first consequence was a war between Sparta and Thebes that arose from a border feud of the Phocians and Locrians. The Thebans, being hard pressed by Lysander from the north and Pausanias from the south, appealed to Athens for help. Lysander was slain in a battle before Haliartus, and Pausanias, on receiving for burial the dead bodies of Lysander and the others, evacuated Boeotia. At this the Spartans were very angry, and Pausanias, to escape their anger, went into voluntary exile. Encouraged by their success, the enemies of Sparta formed a league against her. Thebes, Corinth, Argos, Euboea, joined the alliance, and Sparta was in danger of losing all her empire outside the Peloponnesus. Under these circumstances the Ephors decided to recall Agesilaus.

37. πῶς οὐκ ;] Surely.

(τοῦτ' ἔργον) ὅστις] Namely, that he . . .

Join παραλαβὼν στασιαζούσας : having found them distracted by factions, because of the changes of constitution which had taken place, after the Athenians were deposed from their supremacy.

ἕως αὐτὸς παρῆν] While he was on the spot.

διατελέσαι] With participle, = they continued to be.

38. οὐχ ὡς κ.τ.λ.] A condensed sentence : were grieved at his departure, feeling that it was not a governor only that they were losing, but a father and a friend.

πλαστήν] Predicate. They showed that it was no feigned friendship that they showed ; at any rate they came with him of their own free will to the help of Sparta. Of the two datives, αὐτῷ belongs to the preposition, Λακεδαίμονι to the verb, in συνεβοήθησαν.

οὐ χείροσιν ἑαυτῶν] Men as brave as themselves.

CHAPTER II.

1. While Agesilaus was on his homeward march, the battle of Corinth was fought, July 394. The Lacedaemonians were victorious in their part of the battle, but as their allies were worsted with considerable loss, the victory could hardly be called decisive. At the same time it secured for the time their ascendancy in the Peloponnesus. The allies went home in disgust, and so the confederates on the other side were free to go against Agesilaus.

ὧνπερ] *i.e.* δι' ὧνπερ. ὁ Πέρσης, Xerxes.

τῷ παμπληθεῖ στόλῳ] *The* immense army, for there had been none like it. The army is a kind of instrument, so σύν is omitted.

ἐνιαύσιον] With ἐποιήσατο, predicate : spent a year over.

μεῖον ἢ ἐν μηνὶ = ἐν μείονι ἢ ἐν μηνί. So in *Oeconomic.* xxi. 3 : πλεῖον ἢ ἐν διπλασίῳ χρόνῳ.

οὐ γὰρ ὡς] Apparently οὐ προεθυμεῖτο is used much as οὔ φημι, οὐκ ἐάω. He was anxious not to incur the blame of coming too late for his country's needs. The thought in Xenophon's mind implied some charge or statement, and so he uses the form of oblique statement.

2. ἐξαμείψας] Having quitted Macedonia for Thessaly.

ὅσοι φυγάδες ὄντες ἐτύγχανον] Probably the result of the attempt of Lycophron of Pherae to establish himself as ruler of all Thessaly. XEN. *Hellen.* ii. 3. 4.

ἐκακούργουν] Note the tense : kept constantly harassing them.   •

ἐν πλαισίῳ] In a marching square. The baggage, etc., was put in the centre, and the troops were arranged on the four sides, so that by simply facing round they could meet an attack from any direction.

    Join τοὺς ἡμίσεις τῶν ἱππέων.

τοῦ προηγουμένου στρατεύματος] The van of the army. The tactics here adopted had done good service in the Retreat of the 10,000, and may possibly have been suggested by Xenophon.

3. πρὸς τοὺς ὁπλίτας ἱππομαχεῖν] To fight a cavalry fight in face of the hoplites. That is, they declined the challenge of Agesilaus' cavalry, because the hoplites were there to support them ; and they had no hoplites on their own side.

βάδην] At a walk, slowly.

ἃ ἑκάτεροι ἡμάρτανον] The blunders that both were making, the Thessalians in not getting away, and his own men in not giving chase.

παραγγέλλειν] *sc.* διώκειν. To tell the rest to give chase, and themselves to join in it.

ἀναστροφήν] Time to wheel round.

πλαγίους] Taken in flank.

4. ἐξαίσια] Headlong.

Ναρθακίῳ] Just south of Pharsalus.

5. Πραντός] A town close to Narthacium, position doubtful.

μάλα ἡδόμενος] Much gratified by his success in that, with the cavalry force which he himself had organised, he had beaten men who took a national pride in their horsemanship.

τὰ Ἀχαϊκὰ τῆς Φθίας ὄρη] The mountains of Achaean Phthiotis.

τὴν λοιπὴν] *i.e.* ὁδόν. So PLUTARCH, *Ages.* c. 17, διοδεύσας τὴν Φωκίδα φίλην οὖσαν.

6. Λοκροὺς ἀμφοτέρους] *i.e.* (1.) The Locri Opuntii, or Epicnemidii, who occupied the narrow slip on the eastern coast of Greece from the pass of Thermopylae to the mouth of the Cephissus. Their territory was broken by a narrow strip of Phocian land that stretched down to the Euboean Sea, and contained a seaport, Daphnus. The Locrians north of this were called Epicnemidii, those south of it Opuntii. (2.) The Locri Ozolae, who occupied a district on the Corinthian gulf between Phocis and Aetolia. The two are mentioned separately in the account given in *Hellen.* iv. 2. 17.

μόραν] The citizen army of Sparta was divided into six morae. This mora had come across from Corinth, and the half-mora was from Orchomenus. Plutarch speaks of two morae having joined Agesilaus from Corinth, c. 17.

αὐτόθεν] From the neighbourhood, on the spot. A fuller account of these forces is given in *Hellen.* iv. 3. 15. They consisted of the enfranchised Helots, who had been with him in Asia, Herippidas' band of mercenaries, troops from the Greek cities in Asia, and along his route in Europe.

7. λέξων ἔρχομαι] I am going to say,=λέξειν μέλλω. So in *Anab.* vii. 7. 17, and *Hellen.* iii. 2. 6.

ἐλάττους] Cf. *Hellen.* iv. 3. 15: πελτασταὶ γε μὴν πολὺ πλέονες οἱ μετ' Ἀγησιλάου· ἱππεῖς δὲ αὖ παραπλήσιοι ἀμφοτέροις τὸ πλῆθος.

εἰ γὰρ ταῦτα] For if I were to say this, I should feel that I was making out Agesilaus to be wanting in common sense, and myself to be a fool for praising a man who with such great interests at stake could make such a rash venture.

οὐδὲν μεῖον] This is hardly consistent with the passage from the *Hellenica*, quoted above.

ὡς] Xenophon frequently uses this word for ὥστε.

8. δυνήσοιντο] The past sequence for the future indicative with verbs of caution. *Syntax*, 50, ε.

δέοι] sc. μάχεσθαι, which is repeated from ἱκανοὶ μάχεσθαι.

φιλονεικίαν] Emulation, rivalry.

ἔσοιτο] The direct form would be πολλὰ κἀγαθὰ ὑμῖν ἔσται, ἐὰν ἄνδρες ἀγαθοὶ γίγνησθε.

ἐκ τῶν τοιούτων] With such inducements.

9. καὶ μέντοι] And, to be sure.

Agesilaus, on reaching the Boeotian frontier, had heard of the defeat of the Lacedaemonian fleet at Cnidus (end of July 394 B.C.) and of the death of Pisander, his brother-in-law. (GROTE, ch. 73 end.) Feeling that it was necessary to make the best of the time before his soldiers heard the full details of this disaster, and knowing that, if they believed that Sparta was no longer in the ascendant, they would fall away from him, he determined to hasten the engagement. The enemy were only a day's march from him, so he pushed on with vigour.

Κορώνειαν] Coroneia is situated to the west of Lake Copais in a plain bounded by the river Cephissus on the north, by Mount Helicon on the south, and by Mount Nysaion on the west.

ἑώρων] Xenophon himself was present at this battle. *Anab.* v. 3. 6: ὅτε ἀπῄει σὺν Ἀγησιλάῳ ἐκ τῆς Ἀσίας τὴν εἰς Βοιωτοὺς ὁδόν. PLUTARCH, *Ages.* 18: καὶ παρῆν αὐτὸς (Ξενοφῶν) τῷ Ἀγησιλάῳ συναγωνιζόμενος ἐξ Ἀσίας διαβεβηκώς. It was probably in consequence of this that he was banished from Athens.

ἔσχατοι ἦσαν αὐτῷ τοῦ εὐωνύμου] Were on *his* (αὐτῷ) extreme left.

οἱ δ' αὖ Θηβαῖοι] They were the leaders, and took the right, the most honourable position, themselves (αὐτοί).

10. συνιόντων] *gen. absol.* On their coming together.

δρόμῳ ὁμόσε ἐφέροντο] Charged at the double.

τριῶν πλέθρων] *i.e.* half the distance. The πλέθρον was 100, the στάδιον 600, Greek feet.

11. τῶν Κυρείων τινες] The Greek forces which had returned from Cyrus' expedition. Some of them appear to have taken service under Herippidas, but we may fairly suppose that Xenophon was in command of most of them.

ἐχόμενοι] Next to them.

εἰς δόρυ ἀφικόμενοι] Having crossed spears.

οὐκ ἐδέξαντο] Gave way before.

τῶν ξένων] *i.e.* of Herippidas' force.

ἐστεφάνουν] Were preparing to crown Agesilaus. Their congratulations were premature, for the Thebans had proved superior to the troops opposed to them. Agesilaus had as yet had no experience of the Thebans' bravery, and wishing to prevent the army from rallying, and uniting with those who had already fled, turned to attack them directly.

ἐξελίξας] Having extended his line by bringing up the rear-rank men.

πρὸς τῷ Ἑλικῶνι] The dative implies that they had fled thither, and halted there.

διαπεσεῖν] To force their way through.

12. ἀναμφιλόγως] Past gainsaying.

οὐ μέντοι κ.τ.λ.] But, brave as he was, he did not choose the safest course : he might have let them pass, and then, keeping up the pursuit, have overpowered their rear ; but instead of doing this, he charged them front to front.

Xenophon fails to see that he could not have pursued them far, with their comrades posted on Helicon.

ἐωθοῦντο] They had thought that their weight would carry back the Thebans, but at first it was themselves that were thrust back by the deep phalanx of the Thebans, and they had a hard hand-to-hand fight. Longinus justly praises this passage, which occurs *verbatim* in *Hellen.* iv. 3. 19, as a piece of sublime description. The verbs piled on each other are very expressive.

κραυγή] There was no regular war-cry, but such exclamations as the fury of battle naturally gave rise to.

13. ἡ μὲν νίκη] It could hardly be called a decisive victory, seeing that the Thebans had made good their retreat, though with considerable loss from attacks on their rear.

τῷ ναῷ] The shrine of the Itonian Athena which was close to Coronea. PLUTARCH, *Ages.* 19. ὑπὸ denotes that they were seeking the protection of the sanctuary.

οὐκ εἴα] Forbade.

ἐγένοντο] Note the mood : till they actually were in safety.

14. A ghastly picture of the closeness of the fight.

πεφυρμένην] Soaked ; cf. HOM. *Odyss.* ix. 396,

$$\text{αὐτὰρ ὁ μοχλὸν}$$
$$\text{ἐξέρυσ' ὀφθαλμοῖο πεφυρμένον αἵματι πολλῷ.}$$

70

τὰ μὲν χαμαὶ κ.τ.λ.] Some lying on the ground, some plunged in an enemy's body, some still in the owner's hands.   Cf. THUC. i. 138.   ἃ μετὰ χεῖρας ἔχοι, whatever he had in hand.

15. τῶν πολεμίων] Rejected by Schneider and Dindorf, and hardly necessary to the sense.   Plutarch (c. 19) says that though Agesilaus was severely wounded, he did not return to his tent, till he had seen the dead collected within the lines.   This would seem to imply that they were his own dead.   The Thebans asked on the following day for a truce to bury their dead, but that would be accounted for by the fact that the Spartans were masters of the battle-field.   Mr. Grote, however, thinks that the words are to be retained, and that Agesilaus, feeling that the victory was far from decisive, brought the enemy's dead into his own camp, in order to extort from the Thebans what was ordinarily looked upon as a confession of defeat.   This he considers to be borne out by the somewhat ostentatious assertion of victory that was made on the following day : πρωὶ δε κ.τ.λ.

τῷ θεῷ] To Apollo, to whom the song of victory was addressed.   The temple of Delphi was not far off, and Plutarch tells us that immediately after the confirmation of his victory, Agesilaus went to Delphi, at the time of the Pythian games, and consecrated there the tithe of his Asiatic spoils, to the amount of 100 talents.   So also XENOPHON, *Hellen.* iv. 3. 21.

16. ὑποσπόνδους] *Syntax*, 5 d.   This was equivalent to a confession of defeat.

οἴκαδε ἀπεχώρει] He went home, but the issue of the battle had shown him that he was not equal to forcing his way through Boeotia.   The army turned aside into Phocis, and then into Locris, but the Locrians attacked them, and, though beaten back, kept up a hill warfare against them, in which Gylis, who was in command, was slain.   When they joined Agesilaus, he dismissed them to their homes, and himself crossed the Corinthian gulf into the Peloponnesus.   Meanwhile Sparta, while reaping no fruit from the two victories of Corinth and Coroneia, had felt fully the consequences of the defeat at Cnidus.   Their fleet was gone, and Pharnabazus and Conon sailed from one island to another, and from one seaport to another, in the Aegean, to put down the Spartan power.   The Spartans had not won for themselves any popularity, and in the time of their reverses, their allies readily fell away from them, and seized the offers of Pharnabazus, guaranteeing to each city its independence under Persian protec-

71

tion. Abydos alone held firm, under the judicious government of Derkyllidas, who from it held for Sparta the Chersonesus opposite, in spite of all the efforts of Pharnabazus. In the next spring (393 B.C.) the latter, with Conon, sailed across to the Peloponnesus, and ravaged the coasts of Laconia and Messenia, and captured the island of Cythera. Thence they sailed to the Isthmus of Corinth, where they found the old allies still carrying on the war, from Corinth as their base, against the Lacedaemonians at Sicyon. They held the lines across the Isthmus connecting the two ports of Corinth, Lechaeum and Cenchreae, and were thus able to keep the Spartans within Peloponnesus. The common feeling of hostility to Sparta overpowered the old dislike of Persian influence, and Pharnabazus, at his departure, left with them a considerable sum of money to aid them in their defence. Pharnabazus returned home, but Conon remained, and with him the Persian fleet. With the consent of Pharnabazus, to whom he had pointed out that there could be no severer blow to Sparta than the restoration of Athens, he set to work to rebuild the Long Walls that connected that city with the Piraeus, and the very enemies who had danced with joy eleven years before, when the former walls were destroyed, volunteered their aid. ' If the Spartans had been able to force the lines at the Isthmus, or if Conon had not been there to repel any attack by sea, such a restoration would have been impossible; but it was not till the following year that they ventured to attempt the former of these operations. In the meantime a desultory warfare was going on in the Corinthian territory, and the farmers were anxious to renew the old alliance with Sparta. The government, suspecting this, introduced a body of Argives into the city, and with great cruelty massacred most of their opponents. After this they formed a close alliance with Argos, and removed even the boundary marks between the two States. The aristocratic party at Corinth, dissatisfied with this, admitted the Lacedaemonians inside the long walls that led from Corinth to Lechaeum. A battle took place within these walls, in which the Lacedaemonian force was victorious, and Praxitas, their commander, destroyed a great part of the wall (392 B.C.). Later the Athenians came to their help, and the walls were rebuilt; but the step was rendered useless by Agesilaus taking the field (391).

τὰ νόμιμα δὲ ἄρχεσθαι] In his submission to public discipline, and to the commands of the Ephors.

17. τὰ μὲν οἴκοι] They were unmolested at home, and had added

Corinth to their empire. Xenophon implies that Corinth had become a dependency of Argos (*Hellen.* iv. 4. 6, Ἄργος ἀντὶ Κορίνθου τὴν πατρίδα αὐτοῖς ὀνομάζεσθαι).

αὐτῶν] *sc.* τῶν Ἀργείων.

τὰ στενὰ] *Hellen.* iv. 4. 19, κατὰ Τενέαν.   Pausanias calls the pass πύλην Τενεατικήν.

ἀναπετάσας] Having thrown open.

'Υακίνθια] The Hyacinthia was a great national festival, celebrated every year at Amyclae, by the Amyclaeans and Spartans jointly. It was held in honour of the Amyclaean Apollo, and of the hero Hyacinthus, on the longest day of the month Hecatombeus, when the sun was hottest.   On the first and third days sacrifices were offered to the dead, accompanied by dirges and funereal laments. On the second day, however, the chief day of the feast, there was nothing but rejoicing and amusements.   There was a horse-race, followed by a singing of the paean and of national songs, and by a procession of maidens riding in chariots of wicker-work.

ὅπου ἐτάχθη] Another instance of his submission to discipline.

18. Πειραίῳ] A fortified town on the peninsula, which juts out between Lechaeum and the Alcyonian gulf, N.E. of Corinth.   Opposite it was the Boeotian port of Creusis, so that the Boeotians could easily cross the gulf to come to the help of Corinth.   The peninsula itself is sometimes called by the same name.

ὑπὸ πολλῶν] Including Iphicrates the Athenian, and his peltasts. Finding the place thus strongly defended, Agesilaus returned suddenly to Corinth in the hope of surprising it, while the defenders were so few, and the citizens were keeping the Isthmian games.   The Corinthians, in their alarm, sent for Iphicrates from Peiraeum ; and Agesilaus, learning that these troops had passed, marched back again thither secretly (ὑποστρέψας), and, attacking the place on two sides, got possession of it (B.C. 390).

ὡς ἐνδιδομένης τῆς πόλεως] *sc.* Κορίνθου, 'as if Corinth was on the point of surrendering, after the morning meal he moved his camp up to the city.'

19. ἔρημον φυλακῆς] The garrison and the people had fled to the Heraeum, or sacred enclosure of Hera, near the west end of the peninsula.

20. μετὰ δὲ ταῦτα] This was at the end of the same summer, or at the beginning of 389.   Agesilaus had left Corinth in humiliation. When the Amyclaeans went home to keep the Hyacinthia, a mora of 600 Lacedaemonian hoplites and a small detachment of cavalry were sent with them as an escort. The hoplites returned, leaving the Amyclaeans near Sicyon, and without any suspicion of danger to themselves on the way back. But when Iphicrates saw that they were unsupported by any cavalry, he sallied out from Corinth with his peltasts to waylay them, and was so successful in repeated attacks, that all but a very few were slain ; and their commander sued for a truce to bury the dead. That a regiment of heavy-armed Spartan troops should thus be beaten by a light-armed force was a blow to Spartan prestige which was very keenly felt, and Agesilaus retired to Sparta, hurrying his march to the uttermost, and not halting at any city for fear of insult.

προθύμων ὄντων] So eager were they for it, that they threatened to desert it altogether if the Lacedaemonians did not assist them to secure Kalydon, a dependency of theirs in Aetolia, against the neighbouring Acarnanians.

ἐπιθεμένων] This was in the return march. The Acarnanians gathered in their cities, and sent off their cattle and their goods to the hill-country far inland. Agesilaus by a forced march surprised the place where they had been stored. On his return he met with constant opposition in the narrow passes of the hill-country, which he was able to defeat ; but he could not conquer their cities, and gave up a war which was but of little profit. Still, as the event proved, it was not fruitless, for the Acarnanians sent to Sparta to ask for peace, and agreed to cease from hostilities against the Achaeans. The tactics that he pursued in this mountain warfare recall the account that Xenophon gives in the fourth book of the *Anabasis* of the march of the Ten Thousand through Kurdistan.

'Αργείους] The people of Argos Amphilochicum, to the north of Aetolia. The words that follow cannot refer to Argos in the Peloponnesus.

21. τῇ εἰρήνῃ] The (well-known) peace of Antalkidas—or possibly the article may only refer back to εἰρήνης.

In the three last years that followed this last named exploit of Agesilaus, a change had come over the position of affairs in the east. The Athenian fleet under Thrasybulus had become masters of the Hellespont, and had re-established the old tolls in favour of Athens. The Spartans in their annoyance at this sent out Anaxibius to take the place of Derkyllidas, who, they thought, might have checked the progress of Thrasybulus. Anaxibius failed however, and Antalkidas was sent out (B.C. 388) as Lacedaemonian admiral to Asia to enter into negotiation with Tiribazus the Persian satrap. In the following year he went up to the Persian Court at Susa, and, aided by Tiribazus' influence, won over the king Artaxerxes to his side. He returned bearing the king's proclamation of the terms of peace, which claimed for himself all the cities in Asia and in Cyprus, all other Hellenic cities to remain independent, with the exception of Lemnos, Imbros, and Skyros, restored to Athens. The Spartans were to be responsible for the execution of this treaty. The Thebans tried to override the independence clause by claiming to take the oath on behalf of the Boeotian cities. It was this that Agesilaus so strongly opposed, and he appears to have added also a compulsory clause, restoring those exiles who had been fighting with him on the side of the Lacedaemonians against their own people.

Φλιασίων] These exiles had been recalled at the bidding of Sparta, but on their return the promises that had been made of the restitution of their property were not kept, and the exiles appealed to Sparta. This only aggravated the feeling against them as unpatriotic, and they were fined for the act. Agesilaus took up their cause, and, refusing all overtures on the way, blockaded the town. The people held out for more than a year, but famine at last compelled them to yield. A new government was imposed on them, taken equally from the exiles and from those in the city, and a garrison left for six months, to secure the execution of these terms. Phlius is in Argolis, south-west of Corinth.

ἀλλ' οὖν φιλεταιρίᾳ γε] Xenophon, fond as he is of praising Agesilaus, feels that these harsh measures can hardly be justified—'but at any rate it follows (οὖν) that they were due to his attachment to his partisans.'

22. τοὺς ἐν Θήβαις] About the year 392 B.C. the Chalkidian city of Olynthus became the head of a confederacy of the neighbouring Greek towns for mutual defence against the Illyrians. The people of Acanthus and Apollonia refused to join this confederacy, and on the Olynthians threatening them with war, they sent envoys to Sparta to ask for help (B.C. 383). The Spartans voted an army of 10,000 men, but, as they could not all be got ready at once, Phoebidas, the brother of Eudamidas the general, waited behind to collect the rest of the troops, and marched north through Boeotia. He halted not far from Thebes, and was met, probably by previous arrangement, by the leaders of the Laconian party in Thebes. With their aid he treacherously seized the Cadmea, the

acropolis of Thebes (382 B.C.). The Spartans censured and dismissed him for the act, but did not remove their garrison from the Cadmea. For three years Thebes was a dependency of Sparta. Three hundred of the leaders of the patriotic party fled to Athens. Among these was Pelopidas, and he opened a secret correspondence with his friends in Thebes, which ended in a plot for the assassination of the two polemarchs and for the restoration of liberty to Thebes. The plot was successful : Epaminondas and the other exiles returned. The Lacedaemonian garrison was allowed to withdraw, but some of the citizens of the Laconian party were put to death. An army was sent out against the city from Sparta under king Cleombrotus in the winter, but it did nothing. Again in 379 Agesilaus invaded Boeotia with the full force of the Spartan confederacy, but after a month spent in ravaging the country round Thebes he withdrew to Thespiae, not venturing upon an open battle. In the following year he made a second expedition, but it was equally indecisive, and indeed its only effect was to train the Thebans in military practice and to give them confidence in facing the Spartans. An accident in this campaign incapacitated him for active service for some time.

Κυνὸς κεφαλὰς] A range of hills between Thebes and Thespiae.

Σκῶλον] A small town on the river Asopus under Mount Cithaeron. The palisade probably extended from the mountain to the river.

23. ἐγένοντο] The plural marks the number; cp. XEN. *Anab*. i. 7. 17, ἦσαν ἴχνη πολλά.

ἡγουμένου] Under Agesilaus' leadership. He was laid aside by the accident above named, which had become serious from bad medical treatment.

τῆς ἐν Λεύκτροις συμφορᾶς] In the year 371 a peace was made between Sparta and Athens and their allies, called the peace of Callias, but Agesilaus excluded the Thebans from it because they once more claimed the headship of Boeotia. In consequence of this Cleombrotus, who was in Phocis with a Lacedaemonian army, invaded Boeotia. Epaminondas and Pelopidas stirred up the Thebans to a vigorous resistance. A battle was fought on the plain of Leuctra three weeks after the exclusion of the Thebans from the peace, and the Thebans were victors. The battle was made memorable by the introduction of the manœuvre, so much used in our own day by Napoleon, of concentrating his troops on one point of the enemy's line, and carrying one part of the position by sheer weight. This defeat was truly a 'disaster' for Sparta. Its prestige was gone, and Thebes became for a time supreme. The Peloponnesian cities at once threw off their old mistress, and a new Peloponnesian confederacy was formed, with Athens for its head. The Arcadians were especially affected by the change. Mantinea had been dismantled by the Spartans, and now decided to rebuild its walls. The other cities aimed at an Arcadian confederacy, but Tegea and Orchomenus opposed it, the former being ruled by an oligarchy in the Spartan interest. A good many, however, of the Tegean people were keen for the Pan-Arcadian league, and appealed to an armed public assembly. The oligarchical party got the better of it, till assistance came to the other side from Mantinea, which made them the stronger party. The leaders of the Spartan faction were obliged to surrender, and being put on their trial were condemned and put to death. The Spartans resolved, in spite of their weakness, to make an effort to stay the revolutionary movement, and Agesilaus went out with a Lacedaemonian force, hoping to be joined by a mercenary force from Orchomenus (370 B.C.). The latter, however, had been attacked and defeated by the Mantineans, and he had to advance alone. He encamped within two miles from Mantinea, where his allies from Orchomenus joined him, but where he also found the whole Arcadian force united. He remained there for three days, being at one time in a somewhat critical position, but as the enemy did not leave their walls he fell back to Tegea, and then to Sparta. And Xenophon thinks this a matter to boast of.

24. Epaminondas had resolved to support the Arcadian union, and to restore the exiled Messenians, and accordingly marched into Arcadia late in the autumn of 370, shortly after Agesilaus had left it. There he was joined by the Argives and the Eleans, who urged him to invade Laconia, backing up their entreaty by an invitation from some of the Perioeci.

τῶν δούλων] The Helots.

περιοικίδων] The Perioeci were the descendants of the original Achaean inhàbitants of the land, who formed the Spartan heavy-armed force. They were politically subject to the Spartans, but personally free. They were distributed into 100 townships, and had all the trade and commerce of Laconia in their hands.

καὶ ταῦτα ἀτείχιστον οὖσαν] And that, though it had no walls. The passes leading into the valley of the Eurotas were so easily defensible, that Sparta was always an open town.

ὅπου μὲν κ.τ.λ.] Wherever the enemy would have had the best of it in every way, he refused to lead out his men, but wherever his own people were likely to have the advantage, he confidently offered battle, thinking that if he went out into the open he would be surrounded on all sides, whereas, if he awaited their attack in the more confined and rugged ground, he would have every advantage over them.

τῷ παντί] Dative of measure. *Syntax*, 19 *b*.

25. ἀπεχώρησε] Agesilaus' efforts were successful. Epaminondas' cavalry were repulsed, and he abandoned all further attempt on the city, and returned to Arcadia, after devastating the whole valley of the Eurotas down to the sea.

εὐγνωμόνως χρῆσθαι ἑαυτῷ] He behaved with good judgment. Pres. infin. relatively to φαίη.

χρημάτων δὲ κ.τ.λ.] And saw that the city must have money, if it was to have any allies.

καιρὸς ἦν] *sc.* μετιέναι.

ἀντὶ στρατηγοῦ] Instead of as a general.

26. Autophradates was satrap of Lydia, who, acting upon the king's instructions, was trying to subdue those who had revolted (about 366 B.C.). Ariobarzanes was satrap of Phrygia, Cotys of Paphlagonia, Mausolus of Caria. Little is known of the particulars.

CORN. NEPOS (*Timotheus*, c. 1.) confirms Agesilaus' help to Ariobarzanes; saying of Timotheus, 'Ariobarzani simul cum Agesilao auxilio profectus est.'

τρόπαιον τῶν πολεμίων] A trophy of victory over enemies. τρέπω, to rout; a memorial of the rout of the enemy.

οὐκέτι δείσας, ἀλλὰ πεισθείς] Not in his case through fear, but through persuasion.

27. εὖ πεπονθέναι ὑπ' αὐτοῦ] That they had received good services from him. οἱ φεύγοντες, they who fled from him.

προπομπήν] Escorting, escort.

28. τὸν Αἰγυπτίων βασιλέα] The Tachos just mentioned. He had intended to help the other princes, but their combination had been broken by the Persian court.

29. ἀνθ' ὧν εὐεργετήκει] They had applied to a former Egyptian king for help in the naval war, and had received 100 triremes and 600,000 bushels of corn.

ἐλευθερώσειν] The same peace of Antalkidas which placed the Greek cities in Asia in the Persian power, by its other clause freed Messene from its allegiance to Sparta.

78

30. οὐκ ἀπεδίδου] The Egyptians were disgusted when they found that the hero whom they had invited was a mean-looking, lame, old man, who kept up no apparent dignity. So Agesilaus, instead of being commander-in-chief, as had been promised, was only made commander of the mercenary troops.

οἱ δίχα στρατευόμενοι] Nectanebis, the cousin of Tachos, had been left in charge at home, when the latter, with Agesilaus, started on an expedition against the Persians in Phoenicia. He proclaimed himself king, and the rest of the Egyptians also who were with him abandoned Tachos. He applied to Agesilaus, through Chabrias the Athenian, for help, but he refused to change till he had consulted the government at home. The two rival kings applied to the Lacedaemonians, who left the matter in Agesilaus' hands, directing him secretly to do what should appear most advantageous for Sparta.—PLUT. *Ages.* 37.

διττούς] Another competitor for the attacked throne appeared in the Mendesian division of Egypt.

31. ἀγορὰν δὲ οὐδέτερος παρέξει] And so his troops would not only lose their pay, but be in danger of starving.

32. εἰ δὲ τῷ ἑτέρῳ κ.τ.λ.] But that if he should side with one of the two, he at any rate, in return for his help, would naturally be his friend ; so having made up his mind which of the two seemed more likely to favour the Greeks, he vanquished and subdued the Greek-hater, and helped to set the other on the throne. τὸν ἕτερον, Nectanebis.

ἀργὸς] Idle, for lack of supplies.

CHAPTER III.

1. μετὰ πλείστων μαρτύρων] In the company, *or* in the sight, of very many witnesses. For such things require no confirmatory evidence ; the mere recalling of them is sufficient to secure their immediate acceptance.

ἀρετὴ = Lat. *virtus*, manly character.

δι' ἣν ταῦτα ἔπραττε] Which led him habitually to act (*imperfect*) thus, and to love all that is noble, and to scout all that is mean and degrading.

2. ὡς means more than ὥστε. The proof or the measure of his piety is seen in the trust reposed in him by his enemies.

τὴν ἑαυτῶν φιλίαν] Their friendship among themselves.

οἱ μὲν ὤκνουν] There seems to be something missing here. Schneider inserts συντιθέμενοι ἀλλήλοις τὰ πολλὰ μὲν ὤκνουν. Still the words

79

make sense. For they shrank in the one case from a personal meeting (fearing, that is, that they might be made prisoners or hostages, as the Greek officers with Cyrus were by Tissaphernes), but they fearlessly put themselves in the hands of Agesilaus.

3. γῆμαι ἔπραττε] Was negotiating a marriage with.

τὴν δὲ αὐτοῦ] By Agesilaus' advice, she was married to the Cotys of sect. 4, who is in the *Hellen.* (iv. 1. 3) called Otys.

4. δεξιὰν πέμποντι] Though he sent him a pledge of friendship. Cp. *Anab.* ii. 4. 1, δεξιὰς παρὰ βασιλέως φέροντες. TACITUS, *Hist.* ii. 8, Dextras, concordiae insignia, exercitus nomine ferre.

πελτοφόρους = πελτασtάs.

5. καὶ Φαρνάβαζος] The story is told in *Hellen.* iv. 1. 29 foll. After Agesilaus had overrun Pharnabazus' territory and his residences (see ch. 1.) a man of Cyzicus, named Apollophanes, brought them together, and after a conference they parted as friends.

δὴ] In particular.

εἶναί τε καὶ ὄντα ἐγνῶσθαι] To be, and to be recognised as being.

CHAPTER IV.

1. στέρεσθαι] Being kept out of his own.

ἐνεκάλεσεν] Laid a claim, made it the ground of a claim at law.

ἀποστερεῖν] Technically used of keeping back from a man what you hold in trust for him. 'When a man finds pleasure in giving away what is his own to benefit others, how could he at the same time bring himself to defraud others, with infamy for his only reward? if he were ruled by lust of gold, it were a far easier plan to keep what he had, than to take what does not belong to him.'

ἐφ' ᾧ κακόδοξος εἶναι = ita ut infamis esset. *Syntax*, 49, a.

2. ἂν οὐκ εἰσὶ δίκαι] For which no action can lie. This keeps up the allusion to the legal sense of ἀποστερεῖν, for which a man could be sued in the law-courts, as Demosthenes sued his guardian Aphobus.

κωλύει] sc. ἀποστερεῖν.

τὸ μὴ πολὺ μείζους κ.τ.λ.] That a man who had greater resources should not repay the favours done to him with considerable interest ; *lit.* should not repay much greater favours.

3. τὰς ὀφειλομένας] What was due as a debt of personal gratitude to himself. The general expression is attracted into the gender of χάριτας.

ἐγκρατείας χρημάτων] Of self-control in the matter of money. The expression is closely condensed. The fact that he was able to get

80

money from others proves that he must have been very liberal, and that they must have been making a return for previous gifts from him.

4. εἰ γὰρ ἐπώλει] For if he had been in the habit of selling.

παρακαταθήκην] To guard a kindness, as a deposit, to be returned when required. The word is used of a deposit in a bank, of which an account has to be rendered. It is one of the things to which the word ἀποστερεῖν applies.

5. σὺν τῷ γενναίῳ μειονεκτεῖν] To preserve his honour, though at some sacrifice; *lit.* to lose with honour.

τοίνυν] In proof of it.

6. Τιθραύστου] The man who was sent down to put Tissaphernes out of the way. He called on Agesilaus, promising him large sums (χρήματα διδούς, PLUTARCH, *Ages.* 10) to quit Asia Minor, since his great foe Tissaphernes was dead. When Agesilaus replied that he must wait for instructions from home, he got him to cross over into Pharnabazus' satrapy, and gave him thirty talents for his commissariat ·(*Hell.* iii. 4. 26. There is no mention there of any personal bribe to Agesilaus).

CHAPTER V.

1. σίτων δ' ὑπὲρ καιρὸν κ.τ.λ.] And of excessive eating or too long continued idleness.

οὐχ ὅπως] So far from using both, he sent them about, and did not leave himself either share. οὐχ ὅπως is a condensed expression with ἐρῶ omitted, like the Latin *non dicam, ne dicam.*

πλησμονῆς ἕνεκα] For his own satisfaction.

ὅπως ἔχοι] That he might have the means of honouring therewith any one that he would.

2. ἀρχομένῳ ὑπὸ πραξέων] Regulated by business.

τῶν συνόντων φαυλοτάτην] Meaner than his suite had. The construction is the same as the Latin.

3. τάδε] The neut. accusative is often used as an accusative of the contents of the verb (*Syntax* 13) where the expression is general, though in a particular reference another case is used, as here the genitive.

παρὰ τοὺς ἄλλους] In excess of the rest.

προσίετο] As we say—did not affect ease.

81

CHAPTER VI.

1. **τῇ πόλει**] In the interests of his country.
2. **οὐ φόβῳ τρεψάμενος**] Not routing them by mere fear, *i.e.* by superiority of numbers, or overwhelming force.

   ἀντιτύπῳ μάχῃ] Fair, equally matched, fight. For a victory of this kind he could erect a trophy; the former was merely gaining a chance victory (*νίκης ἔτυχεν*).

   μνημεῖα] In the trophies erected, and in the fruits of his victory; *σημεῖα*, in the honourable scars which he himself had won, which spoke to men's eyes (*ὁρῶντας*) more plainly than any narrative of his exploits (*ἀκούοντας*).

3. **τρόπαια μὴν**] And yet not merely his actual victories, but all his campaigns may be counted as his trophies. Many a bloodless victory he gained by the enemy's unwillingness to face him.

   καὶ ἐν τοῖς ἀγῶσι δὲ] Just as in the public games.

   ἀκονιτὶ] Without raising the dust, without competition; as we should say, 'he who walks over the course receives the prize.'

4. **[αὐτῇ ποιεῖν ὃ βούλοιτο]** It is evident that some words have dropt out after *πειθόμενος*. I have supplied the words in brackets from a passage in Plutarch which appears to refer to this passage, (*Ages.* iv.) ὃ δέ φησιν ὁ Ξενοφῶν, ὅτι πάντα τῇ πατρίδι πειθόμενος ἴσχυε πλεῖστον, ὥστε ποιεῖν ὃ βούλοιτο, τοιοῦτόν ἐστι.

   ἀπροφασίστους] Hearty, never making excuses to shirk duty.

   πῶς ἂν κ.τ.λ.] The two elements of success for an army are good discipline, which respect for their leader enforces, and the hearty confidence which affection for him inspires.

5. **ψέγειν**] Depreciate.

   τοὺς γὰρ συμμάχους] The subject to *πλέον ἔχειν*, the whole clause being the object to *ἐμηχανᾶτο*.

   λήθων] Poetic form of *λανθάνω*,—doing things unobserved.

6. **ἄδηλος γιγνόμενος**] Keeping secret, not betraying.

   τὰ μὲν παριὼν] Passing some by, *i.e.* boldly leaving them in his rear : *ὑπερβαίνων*, passing over them; of mountain passes or barriers of that kind; *κλέπτων*, occupying by stealth, as Xenophon did the pass of the Kiretschli Dagh, *Anabasis*, iv. 6. 11.

7. **ἐξείη τοῖς πολεμίοις**] It was in the enemy's power.

   τό τε ἀτρεμές] The *τε* is a difficulty. It seems better to adopt

Weiske's suggestion—τό τε ἀτρεμὲς καὶ τὸ ἀνέκπληκτον. Thinking that in such a case calmness and freedom from panic causes least confusion, and least blundering, and least liability to secret attack.

8. **θάρσος καὶ ῥώμην ἐνεποίει**] Inspired them with boldness and vigour.

ὥστε κ.τ.λ.] And so his enemies could not despise him, his countrymen could not inflict any penalties upon him.

διετέλεσεν] *sc.* ὤν. He continued to be.

CHAPTER VII.

1. **καθ' ἓν μὲν ἕκαστον**] If one were to write every single detail, it would be a tedious task.

εἰς τοῦτο συντείνει] Has this for its ultimate aim, *lit.* converges to this end.

οὐ πόνων ὑφίετο] Did not shirk any labour.

. **σῶμα**] He was lame, but never alleged that as a reason for evading duty.

2. **δυνατώτατος ὢν κ.τ.λ.**] Though he was the most powerful man in the state, he was conspicuously the most submissive to law.

τίς δ' ἂν κ.τ.λ.] 'Or who would have attempted any revolution, from the idea that his position was below his merits, when he saw that even his king was content to submit to a legal superior?' The ephors at Sparta were able in many cases to control the king.

προσεφέρετο] He bore himself as a father to his children.

3. **ἐλοιδορεῖτο**] Used to chide them, take them to task.

παρίστατο] Used to stand by them.

ζημίαν δὲ τιθείς] Putting it to the account of loss.

ὅταν οἱ Ἕλληνες σωφρονῶσιν] 'When the Greeks are in their senses,' and cast aside their long-continued dissensions. The graphic sequence implies that such a thing is possible.

4. **ἢ πόλιν οὐκ ἐθέλοντα αἱρεῖν**] Either unwilling to capture a town when he thinks he shall have to give it up to pillage, or thinking a victory in a war with Greeks to be a dire calamity.

5. **τῇ ἐν Κορίνθῳ μάχῃ**] See Note on Chapter ii. § 1.

6. **ἐνδιδοῖτο**] Was ready to surrender. See Chapter ii. 18.

σωφρονίζειν] To bring to reason.

ὁρᾶν χρὴ κ.τ.λ] We consider whether we shall not be depriving ourselves of all means of overcoming the foreigner.

7. ὁ πάλαι] *sc.* Πέρσης, understood from μισοπέρσης, Xerxes; ὁ νῦν, Artaxerxes II.

λαβόντας] When they have received his presents.

εἰρήνην] The peace of Antalkidas. See Note on Chapter ii. § 21.

μὴ ἀπόληται] The contingency, as dependent upon their first revolting, is more remote than that of the revolt : hence the subjunctive.

κακὰ ἔχων] Being occupied with troubles of his own.

ἐξέπλευσεν] When he went to Egypt.

CHAPTER VIII.

1. τὸ εὔχαρι] His urbanity.

ᾧ γε] Strictly dependent on ὑπαρχούσης, but may be taken also with εἶδεν ἄν, 'in whom.'

τῶν φίλων] Objective genitive, after the transitive idea of θεραπευτικόν.

καὶ μὴ ζητῶν] Even without looking for it.

2. μὴ] Because πλησιάζειν is consecutive. To consort with him, seek his presence, not only for the sake of getting something out of him, but to add pleasure to their daily life.

οἶος μεγαληγορεῖν] Given to boasting.

ὑπισχνεῖσθαι] Their self-commendation was a pledge that their actions should not belie it.

3. μεγαλογνωμοσύνῃ] Loftiness of sentiment, high principle.

Καλλία] Elsewhere called Καλλίας.

ἰδίᾳ μὲν] To him in his personal capacity.

ὅτι καὶ αὐτός] The ὅτι, like our 'he said,' reminds us that it is a quotation.

ἀνὰ κράτος] To the utmost of his power.

4. πρὸς] In comparison with.

τούτῳ κ.τ.λ.] That he should be more proud.

5. τῆς προνοίας] Gen. after ἐκεῖνο. That feature of foresight in him : that quality of his foresight.

ξενωθῆναι αὐτῷ] To enter into the tie of a guest-friend with him.

ἐθελῆσαι is consecutive. He was not induced to consent.

6. ἐκεῖνο] That other point, explained by what follows.

ἀντεσκευάσατο] Furnished in contrast (to the Persian king).

7. τὰς θύρας] Here, of the actual door. The Lacedaemonians ascribed the origin of their monarchy to Aristodemus himself, not to his sons.— HEROD. vi. 52.

ἐθοίναζε] Cf. v. 1.

πολιτικοῦ κανάθρου] Public conveyance. The κάναθρον was apparently a carriage made of wicker-work. In Homer it is called πείρινς.

εἰς Ἀμύκλας] To celebrate the Hyacinthia.

8. ταῖς προσόδοις] His income.

καλὸν μὲν κ.τ.λ.] Translate: If it is thought a noble thing to win positions that are impregnable by an enemy, I, for my part, think it a far nobler thing to make one's soul impregnable by any force of bribery, or pleasure, or fear.

CHAPTER IX.

1. τὸν τρόπον ὑπεστήσατο] Made his manner of living a contrast to the haughty pomp of the Persian king.

τῷ σπανίως ὁρᾶσθαι ἐσεμνύνετο] Piqued himself on being rarely seen ; or, possibly, won for himself awe by rarely showing himself. The former rendering makes the best contrast to ἠγάλλετο.

αἰσχρουργίᾳ] Men 'love darkness better than light, because their deeds are evil.'

τυχόντας ὧν δέοιντο] With their requests granted.

3. εὐπαθείαν] Comfort.

μαστεύοντες] Seeking out—a poetical word.

ὅσα πραγματεύονται] How many devices they invent.

πᾶν τὸ παρὸν] All that came to hand.

4. ἐν μέσαις ταῖς εὐφροσύναις] In the midst of his delights; they were on the spot, because he could take contentedly just what came to hand.

τὸν δὲ βάρβαρον] After a common Greek idiom, the word, which belongs to the subordinate clause, becomes the object of the principal, as οἶδά σε, τίς εἶ, I know who thou art.

5. τῇ τῶν θεῶν κατασκευῇ] 'The gods' arrangement' of the seasons, as appears from what follows, and from PLUT. *Ages.* 14, ὥσπερ μόνος ἀεὶ χρῆσθαι ταῖς ὑπὸ θεοῦ κεκραμέναις ὥραις πεφυκώς.

85

6. **ἐπιδεῖξαι νικώσης αὐτῆς**] And showed by her victory.

τὸ θρέμμα τοῦτο] As opposed to the war-horse. If women could train them for the race, it was merely a sign of wealth.

7. **πρὸς τὸ γενναῖον**] Nobly, by the standard of nobleness.

κεκτῇτο] A recognised form of the opt. of κέκτημαι; cf. SOPH. *Phil.* 119.

νικῴη εὐεργετῶν] Surpass every one in his good deeds to his country.

νικηφόρος ἀγωνισμάτων] As compared with victors in the races.

ὀνομαστότατος] This was the chief reward of the conquerors in the games : it won for them great consideration at home.

CHAPTER X.

1. **ταῦτα γὰρ**] *sc. ἐστίν.* For this is not a case like that of a man finding a chance treasure, which makes him richer, but not necessarily a better manager ; nor like that of a commander who gains an advantage over an enemy smitten by some epidemic, who may claim the credit of good fortune, but not that of improved generalship ; on the contrary (δὲ), the man who shows the most endurance where toil is required, and the most valour in a struggle of bravery, and the most judgment where counsel is needed, he, methinks, may fairly be called a perfect man.

2. **καλὸν εὕρημα**] A good find, a godsend.

σταθμή] A standard and rule to measure brave deeds.

δίκαιον] *sc. μιμούμενος.* So σώφρονα.

γὰρ] He was ἐγκρατής, for, etc.

πρὸς is used in slightly different senses : up to the enemy, *i.e.* against them ; up to a perfect ideal, *i.e.* to a goal.

3. **ἀλλὰ μὴ κ.τ.λ.**] But let not any one think that because he is praised now that he is dead, therefore this is a mere funeral elegy, but rather that it is a eulogy. The former would merely recount the virtues of the deceased without any reference to the survivors.

ὡραῖος] (from ὥρα) Timely, ripe, in good old age.

4. **ἐρασθεὶς τοῦ εὐκλεὴς γενέσθαι**] Having set his affection on winning distinction.

τὸ μήκιστον] The longest span allowed to human life.

ἀναμάρτητος] The commentators are much exercised by this expression. Xenophon in his *Hellenica* criticises Agesilaus' mistakes but here, holding him up as an example for imitation, he naturally dwells upon the general perfection rather than the individual flaws.

CHAPTER XI.

1. ὡς ἄν] That so. The ἄν implies that 'in that case' the desired result will follow.

ἱκετὰς δὲ κ.τ.λ.] And he would use no force even to foes when they had taken sanctuary.

ἄλογον] It is the inconsistency between the two (μὲν . . . δὲ) which is unreasonable. Translate, whilst you call . . . to think.

2. ὑμνῶν] Saying over and over again. Lat. *decantare*.

οὐκ ἀνθρώπων ὑπερεφρόνει] He did not look down upon other men (as if it were by his own superiority that he had succeeded), but gave thanks to the gods.

θαρρῶν κ.τ.λ.] He offered more sacrifices (as thank-offerings) in time of success than vows in time of fear.

3. αἰσχροκερδεῖς] Greedy of base gain.

4. ἐξομιλεῖν] To associate with ; χρῆσθαι, to make friends of.

περὶ ὧν λέγοιεν] The character of those about whom they were speaking.

σοφὸν] Good policy. His idea was that if a man plainly mistrusted him, it was quite fair to take him in.

5. ἐπαινούμενος δὲ κ.τ.λ.] He delighted in the praise of those who are willing to find fault with what is unlovely, and never showed dislike for any one who spoke out his mind—but reserved people he watched against, as he would an ambuscade.

τούς γε μὴν διαβόλους]

     ' Who steals my purse steals trash ; . . .
     But he who filches from me my good name
     Robs me of that which not enriches him,
     And makes me poor indeed.'—*Othello*, Act. iii. Sc. 3, l. 157.

6. οὐ ῥᾳδιουργίαν] Not facility (which implies recklessness), but noble-ness and high principle.

7. εἰκόνα στήσασθαι] To let any statue of himself be erected (note the middle). PLUTARCH, *Ages.* 2, τῆς δὲ μορφῆς εἰκόνα οὐκ ἔχομεν. He goes on to say that he was a little man, with no commanding aspect.

8. τῷ μὲν δικαίῳ] Thinking that while it might be sufficient for a just man to let his neighbour's goods alone, the liberal man was bound to help him from what he had himself.

τοὺς μὲν καλῶς ζῶντας] Cp. SOPH. *Oed. Tyr.* 1528 :—

> ὥστε θνητὸν ὄντ' ἐκείνην τὴν τελευταίαν ἰδεῖν
> ἡμέραν ἐπισκοποῦντα μηδέν' ὀλβίζειν πρὶν ἂν
> τέρμα τοῦ βίου περάσῃ μηδὲν ἀλγεινὸν παθών.

9. ἧς οὐκ ἐξεπόνει τὰ ἴδια] Of which he did not work out the details. He did not care for any reputation which he had not properly won.

μετ' εὐβουλίας] With soberness, rather than with rashness.

10. καὶ τὸ εὔχαρι] And his urbanity he did not show in jests and jokes, but in the whole character of his life.

τῇ μὲν ἀμφὶ τὸ σῶμα φαυλότητι] At the poverty—or the meanness—of his own appearance : *i.e.* his dress and surroundings were poor and mean.

11. βαρύτατος μὲν κ.τ.λ.] He was a formidable opponent, but always used his victory leniently.

εὐπαραπειστότατος] Easily influenced.

ἀμαυροῦν κ.τ.λ.] He made it his business to impair the interests of his enemy. ἀμαυρόω, *lit.* to blind, obscure.

12. ἀπροφάσιστον] Ready. (ἀ, προφασίζομαι, making no excuses.)

μετὰ θεοὺς] Next to the gods.

13. τῶν ἀγαθῶν ἀνδρῶν] In brave men.

μεγάλην—δόξαν] As ἐφιέμενος generally takes the genitive, and there are lacunae in the MSS., it would be better to read with Breitenbach, οὐκ ἀπεῖπε μεγάλων καὶ καλῶν ἐφιέμενος, ἕως τὸ σῶμα κ.τ.λ. He never gave up the pursuit of high and noble things as long as his physical constitution was equal to the strain of his mental vigour.

14. τὸ μήκιστον] At his most advanced age.

στόματι] The river's mouth is the river's end. Man's life is compared to a river. We imply the same figure when we speak of the ocean of eternity.

15. μεγαλείως ὠφελῶν] By the treasure he was bringing when he died. Cp. ii. 31. Nectanebis had given him 230 talents for the expenses of the war in Greece.—PLUTARCH, *Ages.* 40.

16. εἰς τὴν ἀΐδιον οἴκησιν κατηγάγετο] He returned (κατάγεσθαι, to put into port) to his last home. The expression seems to have been an Egyptian one. His body was embalmed in wax and brought home for burial, CORN. NEPOS, *Ages.* c. 8, and PLUTARCH, *Ages.* 40. He died at the age of more than eighty, on the coast of Africa, at a place called Menelaus' Haven.

The picture that Xenophon gives in this memoir must be accepted with some reservation. He is biassed here, as in the *Hellenica*, by his admiration for the Lacedaemonian system, as well as by strong personal friendship for their king, with whom, as we have seen, he served in one at least of his Grecian campaigns. There is much to admire in Agesilaus' character. He was a brave soldier, and an able commander ; one who by his strong will and personal tact was able to maintain an influence over those with whom he was brought in contact, and that too in spite of his insignificant appearance, heightened by personal deformity. He had all the good qualities of the Spartan—courage, endurance, simple unluxurious habits. He was true to his word, inaccessible to bribes, winning and hearty in manner,—virtues which were not Spartan. He was ambitious, but rather as king of Sparta than as an individual. But on the other hand he was not a statesman. He let himself be carried away by prejudices, and by likes and dislikes, which the true statesman keeps under control. The time of his Asiatic campaigns is the most satisfactory part of his career. A genuine dislike to Persian government and a genuine Greek patriotism were its inspiring motives. But even here he could not rise above the Spartan model, and where the Persian government was abolished, he would set up in its place the harmosts of Sparta, who seldom failed in a few years to make themselves as much hated as the Persian governors had been. When he returned to Europe, the hatred of Persia was succeeded by a still bitterer hatred of Thebes. Plutarch implies that the treacherous seizure of the Cadmea by Phoebidas was of his designing. At any rate, when it had succeeded, he was foremost in persuading the Lacedaemonians to keep what they had thus won, and in endeavouring to screen Phoebidas from punishment. So far was the old feeling forgotten during this period, that he did not hesitate to sacrifice the Asiatic Greeks, and to make Persia the ally of Sparta in order to secure her empire in Greece. Till the return of the exiles to Thebes, Sparta regained her power, but her absoluteness and injustice paved the way for her speedy fall. In the days of her depression, which followed the battle of Leuctra, he stands out again as an energetic and yet cautious leader. Later, when obliged to seek help from abroad, he did good service once more against the Persians, and by establishing Nectanebis as king of Egypt, he freed it for the time being from the Persian sway.

(Chiefly from GROTE, *History of Greece.*)

B.C.

440? Agesilaus born. He died about 360 B.C., and is said to have then been above eighty years of age.

404. Athens taken by the Lacedaemonians under Lysander.

401. Expedition of Cyrus the younger. The Greek mercenaries that accompanied him returned in the following year.

399. Derkyllidas sent out in command of the Lacedaemonian forces to assist the Greek cities in Asia against Tissaphernes and Pharnabazus. Agesilaus made king of Sparta.

396. Agesilaus supersedes Derkyllidas. His first campaign in Asia. Winters at Ephesus.

395. Second campaign in Asia. He defeats Tissaphernes (battle of Sardis), who is superseded and put to death by Tithraustes. The latter stirs up the Greek States in Europe to make war upon Lacedaemon.

394. Agesilaus is recalled. Battles of Corinth and of Coronea. Defeat of the Spartans by sea at Cnidus.

393. Conon restores the Long Walls of Athens and the fortifications of the Peiraeus.

392. The Lacedaemonians pull down the Long Walls between Corinth and Lechaeum.

391. The Athenians restore these walls, which are retaken, and Lechaeum captured by Agesilaus.

390. Agesilaus captures Peiraeum. The Spartan mora cut to pieces by Iphicrates and his peltastes.

390-389. Expedition against Acarnania.

387. Peace of Antalkidas.

386. The Spartans restore Plataea.

385. The Lacedaemonians under Agesipolis destroy Mantinea.

B.C.

383. Sparta declares war upon Olynthus.

382. Phoebidas seizes the Cadmea, and sets up a Lacedaemonian government in Thebes. Agesilaus defends him when impeached for the act.

380. Agesilaus subdues Phlius.

379. Pelopidas and his companions retake the Cadmea and drive out all the Lacedaemonians from Boeotia.

378. Agesilaus marches against Thebes with the full force of the confederacy, but retires after devastating the land.

377. Second expedition of Agesilaus into Boeotia.

371. Peace of Callias, from which Thebes is excluded because it will not acknowledge the independence of the Boeotian towns. Hence a war arises between the Lacedaemonians and the Thebans, in which the latter obtain a decisive victory under Epaminondas at Leuctra.

370. Mantinea restored. Agesilaus marches against it. The Arcadians apply to Thebes for help, and Epaminondas invades the Peloponnesus and founds Megalopolis and Messene. Vigilant defence of Laconia by Agesilaus.

362. Night march of Epaminondas to surprise Sparta. Agesilaus, who had been sent from Sparta to join the forces gathered against the Thebans at Mantinea, by his prompt return saves the city. After this was fought the battle of Mantinea, in which Epaminondas was killed.

362-361. Revolt of Persian satraps in Asia Minor. Tachos, king of Egypt, joins it. Agesilaus goes to Egypt as commander.

360? Death of Agesilaus.

INDICES.

I.—GEOGRAPHICAL AND HISTORICAL.

Acarnania, Agesilaus' campaign in, ii. 20.

Achaei, in possession of Calydon, ii. 20.

Achaean Mountains (Phthiotis), ii. 5.

Aenianes, a Thessalian tribe on the northern slope of Mount Oeta, ii. 6.

Aeolia, a tract of land along the Aegean from the Troad to the river Hermus, i. 14.

Agesilaus, son of Archidamus, i. 5, and *passim.*

Agis, son of Archidamus, and half-brother of Agesilaus, i. 5.

Amyclae, a town of Laconia, on the right bank of the Eurotas and two and a half miles south of Sparta, where the Hyacinthian festival was held, ii. 7, viii. 7.

Antalkidas, the agent in a peace between Sparta and Persia, called by his name (B.C. 387), ii. 4. 19; vii. 7.

Arcadia, the central district of the Peloponnesus.

Archidamus, father of Agis and Agesilaus, king of Sparta, 469-427 B.C., i. 5.

Argos, an old city in Argolis, on the east of Peloponnesus.

Ariobarzanes, Satrap of Phrygia, ii. 26.

Aristodemus, one of the Hera-clidae, father of Eurysthenes and Procles, and founder of the royal house of Sparta, viii. 7.

Artemis, the goddess of the Ephesians, a representation of the fruitfulness of nature, and so quite distinct from the Greek goddess of the same name, v. 27.

Assus, a town of Mysia, on the bay of Adramyttium (Acts xx. 13), ii. 26.

Autophradates, Satrap of Lydia, ii. 26.

Boeotia, a district of northern Greece, between Attica and the Opuntian mountains (south and north) and between Helicon and Parnassus and the Euboic Sea (west and east).

Calleas, a Lacedaemonian, viii. 3.

Caria, the south-west corner of Asia Minor, i. 14.

Cephisus, a river of Boeotia, that rises in Phocis, and, fed by numerous streams, falls into Lake Copais. Thence it passes by a subterranean outlet of four miles to Larymna, and thence in one and a half miles to the sea, ii. 9.

Corinth, on the isthmus that joins the Peloponnesus to the mainland, the scene of a war between Sparta and the Theban confederation, ii. 17.

Coronea, a town in Boeotia, on a

hill at the entrance of one of the valleys leading up to Mt. Helicon. The plain below was the scene of a battle between the Athenians and Boeotians in 447 B.C., of the battle between Thebes and the Spartans under Agesilaus, 394 B.C., and of one of the engagements of the Sacred War under Philip of Macedon, ii. 9.

Cŏtys, Satrap of Paphlagonia, ii. 26.

Crannon, a town of Pelasgiotis in Thessaly, not far from Larissa, ii. 2.

Creusis, the harbour of Thespiae, at the east end of the Corinthian gulf, ii. 8.

Cynisca, a sister of Agesilaus, ix. 6.

Cynoscephalae (the Dog's heads), a mountain ridge between Thebes and Thespiae, ii. 22.

Cyrei (Κυρεῖοι), the Greek soldiers who had accompanied Cyrus the younger, and after their return had remained with their officers as condottieri, ii. 11.

Delphi, a small town of Phocis, on the south slope of Mount Parnassus, the seat of the oracle of Apollo, i. 34.

Elis, the western district of Peloponnesus north of Messenia.

Ephesus, the chief of Ionian cities on the coast of Asia Minor, south of the Cayster river.

Helĭcon, a range of mountains in Boeotia between the lake Copais and the Corinthian gulf.

Helots, the serf class of Laconia. They cultivated the lands of the Spartan citizens, paying a large percentage of the produce as a rent. They had no political privileges, and went out as light-armed troops with their masters, ii. 24.

Herippĭdas, a captain of mercenary troops who served with Agesilaus. ii. 10.

Hyacinthia, a festival held at Amyclae by the Spartans and Amyclaeans jointly. See note on ii. 17.

Larissa, an important town in Thessaly, on the Peneus, ii. 2.

Lechaeum, the port of Corinth on the Corinthian gulf, as Cenchreae was on the Saronic gulf, ii. 17.

Leotychĭdes, the reputed son of Agis, who, being a minor, was rejected as king, owing to suspicions of his legitimacy, i. 5.

Leuctra, a small town of Boeotia, on the road from Plataea to Thespiae, the scene of the battle that transferred the supremacy from Sparta to Thebes (371 B.C.), ii. 24.

Lŏcri, the inhabitants of two districts in continental Greece. Those who dwelt on the east coast opposite Euboea from Thermopylae to the frontiers of Boeotia were called *Locri Opuntii,* and those who dwelt in Western Locris, along the north side of the Corinthian gulf, between Aetolia and Phocis, were known as *Locri Ozolae,* ii. 6. 24.

Maeander, a river that formed the boundary between Lydia and Caria, i. 15.

Mausōlus, Satrap of Caria, ii. 26.

Messēnē, the capital of Messenia, founded by Epaminondas in 369 B.C., after the battle of Leuctra, to be a counterpoise to Sparta, ii. 29. It lay at the foot of Mount Ithōmē, which was its acropolis.

Narthacius, Narthacium, a mountain and a town in Thessaly, south-west of Pharsalus, ii. 4. 5.

II.—GREEK WORDS.

III.—GRAMMATICAL.

EDINBURGH: T. AND A. CONSTABLE, PRINTERS TO HER MAJESTY.